The Portraits of
John Marshall

John Marshall, *ca.* 1797. (See also figure 1)

Mary Willis Marshall (Mrs. John Marshall), 1799. (See also figure 2)

The Portraits of
JOHN MARSHALL

Andrew Oliver

Published for the
Institute of Early American History and Culture
Williamsburg, Virginia

by the University Press of Virginia
Charlottesville

The Institute of Early American History and Culture
is sponsored jointly by
The College of William and Mary in Virginia
and The Colonial Williamsburg Foundation.

The publication of this volume has been assisted by
a grant from the National Historical Publications
and Records Commission.

THE UNIVERSITY PRESS OF VIRGINIA

First published 1977

The ornament on the opposite page is based
upon John Marshall's personal seal, as it appears on a gold watch fob
that also bears the seal of his wife, Mary Willis Marshall.
It was drawn by Richard J. Stinely of Williamsburg, Virginia,
from the original, now owned by
the Association for the Preservation of Virginia Antiquities, Richmond,
and is published with the owner's permission.

Library of Congress Cataloging in Publication Data
Oliver, Andrew, 1906–
    The portraits of John Marshall.

    Includes index.
    1. Marshall, John, 1755–1835—Portraits, caricatures,
etc.—Catalogs.   I.   Institute of Early American History
and Culture, Williamsburg, Va.   II.   Title.
E302.6.M4044   704.94′23′0973   76–13648
ISBN 0–8139–0633–4

Printed in the United States of America

This volume has been prepared under the auspices of
The Papers of John Marshall,
a multivolume publication project sponsored by
The College of William and Mary in Virginia
and the
Institute of Early American History and Culture.

Contents

Acknowledgments   xix

Introduction   1
1. Earliest Likenesses   6
2. The So-Called Houdon Bust   9
3. Charles Balthazar Julien Fevret de Saint-Mémin (1770–
   1852)   18
4. Cephas Thompson (1775–1856)   27
5. Joseph Wood (*ca.* 1778–1830)   35
6. Samuel Finley Breese Morse (1791–1872)   38
7. Edward F. Peticolas (b. 1793)   42
8. The Last Known Likenesses of "Dearest Polly"   45
9. Rembrandt Peale (1778–1860)   48
10. John Wesley Jarvis (1780–1840)   54
11. Chester Harding (1792–1866)   64
12. John Blennerhassett Martin (1797–1857)   83
13. Beverley Waugh–Robert Ball Hughes (1806–1868)   93
14. Robert Matthew Sully (1803–1855)   100
15. George Catlin (1796–1872)   113
16. William Henry Brown (1808–1883)   121
17. Henry Inman (1801–1846)   134
18. William James Hubard (1807–1862)   164
19. John Frazee (1790–1852)   171
20. Miscellaneous and Posthumous Likenesses   179

Index   195

Illustrations

In giving the dimensions of a portrait, height is mentioned first, then width; in certain instances, as in the case of busts or silhouettes, the only dimension given is the height. Measurements "by sight" are used when it has not been possible, because of a frame, to get the exact measurement of the canvas. The word *replica* refers to an artist's own reproduction of his own original work; the term *copy* refers to the reproduction of an artist's work by another. The courtesy lines in the list below normally indicate ownership where known, but in some instances they indicate only the sources of photographs used for reproduction. The text should be consulted for detailed information on ownership and dating.

1. John Marshall. Oil on ivory, artist unknown, *ca.* 1797, 2½ by 2 inches. Courtesy of Mrs. Benjamin T. Woodruff, Charleston, W.Va.   7

2. Mary Willis Marshall (Mrs. John Marshall). Pastel on paper, artist unknown, 1799, 20½ by 16½ inches. Courtesy of William E. Wiltshire III, Richmond.   7

3. Mary Willis Marshall. Oil on ivory, artist unknown, *ca.* 1785–1790, 2½ inches high. Courtesy of the Association for the Preservation of Virginia Antiquities, John Marshall House, Richmond.   8

4. John Marshall. Terra-cotta mask, artist unknown, *ca.* 1797, 5¾ inches high. Courtesy of the Association for the Preservation of Virginia Antiquities, John Marshall House, Richmond.   11

5. John Marshall. Plaster reproduction of figure 4, artist and date unknown, 5¾ inches high. Courtesy of the Virginia Historical Society, Richmond.   12

6. John Marshall. Modified plaster "metalized" reproduction of figure 4, maker and date unknown, approximately 5¾ inches high. Courtesy of the Virginia Historical Society, Richmond.   12

7. John Marshall. Bronze reproduction of figure 4 or figure 6, maker and date unknown, approximately 5¾ inches high. Courtesy of Mrs. Mary Marshall Swann, Baltimore.   13

8. John Marshall. Bronze copy of figure 4 or one of its derivatives by Moreau Vauthier, 1890, approximately 5¾ inches

high. Courtesy of The Johns Hopkins University, Baltimore.   14

9. John Marshall. Bronze bust after figure 4 by Herbert Adams, 1925. Courtesy of the Hall of Fame for Great Americans at New York University, New York City.   17

10. John Marshall. Physiognotrace on paper by Charles Balthazar Julien Fevret de Saint-Mémin, 1808, approximately 20 by 15 inches. Courtesy of Duke University, Durham, N.C.   20

11. John Marshall. Reproduction of figure 10, from photoengraving on copper plate, by Christian Klackner, 1901, 24¼ by 14¾ inches. Courtesy of the Association for the Preservation of Virginia Antiquities, John Marshall House, Richmond.   22

12. John Marshall. Reproduction of figure 10 on behalf of its owner, artist unknown, 1888, approximately 20 by 15 inches. Courtesy of the Philadelphia Bar Association.   22

13. John Marshall. Reproduction of figure 10 engraved by Charles Balthazar Julien Fevret de Saint-Mémin, 1808, approximately 2 inches in diameter. Courtesy of the Corcoran Gallery of Art, Washington, D.C.   24

14. John Marshall. Bronze medal after figure 10 by Karl H. Gruppe, designed for the Hall of Fame for Great Americans, 1965, 1¾ inches in diameter. Courtesy of Andrew Oliver, Boston.   25

15. John Marshall. Oil on canvas by Cephas Thompson, 1809–1810, 27½ by 22½ inches. Courtesy of The Johns Hopkins University, Baltimore.   29

16. John Marshall. Stipple engraving after figure 15 by David Edwin after Jeremiah Paul, 1815, 3⅞ by 3⅛ inches. Courtesy of the Virginia Historical Society, Richmond.   30

17. John Marshall. Oil on canvas after figure 15 by Jane Braddock Peticolas, after 1810, 27 by 22½ inches. Courtesy of Mrs. John M. Gatewood, Jr., Richmond.   32

18. John Marshall. Oil on canvas, replica or copy of figure 15, artist, date, and size unknown. Owner unknown.   32

19. John Marshall. Oil on canvas, replica or copy of figure 15, artist and date unknown, 27¼ by 22½ inches. Courtesy of the Association of the Bar of the City of New York, New York City.   32

20. John Marshall. Oil on canvas, copy of figure 15, artist and date unknown, 26½ by 22 inches. Courtesy of the Association for the Preservation of Virginia Antiquities, John Marshall House, Richmond (on loan from Charles E. A. Marshall).   33

21. John Marshall. Oil on canvas, copy or replica of figure 15,

artist and date unknown, 27 by 22 inches. Courtesy of the Yale University Art Gallery (gift of Mrs. Lynde Selden).   33

22. John Marshall. Stipple engraving by Francis Kearny after Joseph Wood, 1817, 4⅝₁₆ by 3⅞₁₆ inches. Courtesy of The New-York Historical Society, New York City.   36

23. The Old House of Representatives. Oil on canvas by Samuel Finley Breese Morse, 1822, 86½ by 130¾ inches. Courtesy of the Corcoran Gallery of Art, Washington, D.C.   39

24. Detail of figure 23.   40

25. John Marshall. Oil on canvas by Edward F. Peticolas, *ca.* 1824, 36 by 29 inches. Courtesy of Lafayette College, Easton, Pa.   43

26. Mary Willis Marshall. Pen and ink on paper by Thomas Marshall, *ca.* 1820–1830, 4 by 3½ inches. Courtesy of the Association for the Preservation of Virginia Antiquities, John Marshall House, Richmond.   46

27. Mary Willis Marshall. Oil on canvas, copy or replica of figure 24, artist and date unknown, 29½ by 24½ inches. Courtesy of the Association for the Preservation of Virginia Antiquities, John Marshall House, Richmond.   47

28. John Marshall. Oil on canvas by Rembrandt Peale, 1825, 72 by 54 inches. Courtesy of the Supreme Court of the United States, Washington, D.C.   49

29. John Marshall. Engraving, after figure 28, postage stamp, engraver unknown, 1954, ¾ by ⅝ inches. Courtesy of Herbert A. Johnson, Williamsburg, Va.   50

30. John Marshall. Oil on canvas, replica of figure 28, by Rembrandt Peale, date unknown, 30 by 25 inches. Courtesy of the Virginia Museum of Fine Arts, Richmond.   51

31. John Marshall. Oil on canvas by John Wesley Jarvis, *ca.* 1825, 30 by 25 inches. Courtesy of Richard Coke Marshall, Durham, N.C.   56

32. John Marshall. Oil on canvas, replica or prototype of figure 31, by John Wesley Jarvis, date unknown, 30 by 25 inches. Courtesy of Dr. John Marshall Thayer, Hillsborough, Calif.   57

33. John Marshall. Oil on canvas, copy or possibly replica of figure 31, artist and date unknown, 29 by 24 inches. Courtesy of the University Club, New York City.   57

34. John Marshall. Oil on canvas, copy or replica of figure 31, artist and date unknown. Courtesy of the Valentine Museum, Richmond.   59

35. John Marshall. Oil on canvas, replica of figure 31 or one of

its derivatives, by John Wesley Jarvis, date unknown, 30 by 25 inches. Courtesy of the Thomas Gilcrease Institute of American History and Art, Tulsa, Okla.   59

36. John Marshall. Oil on canvas by John Wesley Jarvis, 1825, approximately 30 by 25 inches. Courtesy of the White House Collection, Washington, D.C.   60

37. John Marshall. Etching and engraving, after figure 36, by Albert Rosenthal, *ca.* 1900, 8¾ by 5¾ inches. Courtesy of The New-York Historical Society, New York City.   60

38. John Marshall. Oil on canvas, copy probably of figure 32, artist and date unknown, 29¼ by 24¼ inches. Courtesy of the Association for the Preservation of Virginia Antiquities, John Marshall House, Richmond.   63

39. John Marshall. Oil on canvas, replica with variations of figure 31, by John Wesley Jarvis, date unknown, 30 by 25 inches. Courtesy of Messrs. Carter, Ledyard, and Milburn, New York City.   63

40. John Marshall. Oil on canvas by Chester Harding, 1828, 36 by 27½ inches. Courtesy of the Harvard University Portrait Collection, Cambridge, Mass., bequest of Joseph Story, 1845.   68

41. John Marshall. Oil on canvas by Chester Harding, *ca.* 1829, 30 by 25 inches. Courtesy of Washington and Lee University, Lexington, Va.   69

42. John Marshall. Oil on canvas attributed to Chester Harding, *ca.* 1829, 35¼ by 27¼ inches. Courtesy of Tulane University, New Orleans.   70

43. John Marshall. Oil on canvas, possibly after figure 42 or a modification of figure 44, by John Cranch, date unknown, 30½ by 25¼ inches. Courtesy of Washington University, St. Louis, Mo.   71

44. John Marshall. Oil on canvas by Chester Harding, 1829, 94 by 38 inches. Courtesy of the Boston Athenaeum.   75

45. John Marshall. Etching after figure 44 by Albert Rosenthal, 1904, 18¼ by 14¼ inches. Courtesy of Paul E. Sternberg, Hampton, Va.   81

46. John Marshall. Oil on canvas by John Blennerhassett Martin, *ca.* 1828, 30 by 25 inches. Courtesy of the University of Virginia, Charlottesville.   84

47. John Marshall. Oil on canvas, possibly after figure 49, by James L. Wattles, prior to 1840, size unknown. Portrait destroyed in the 1950s. Photograph courtesy of the Frick Art Reference Library, New York City.   86

48. John Marshall. Oil on canvas by John Blennerhassett Martin, *ca.* 1834, 29½ by 24¼ inches. Courtesy of the Supreme Court of the United States, Washington, D.C. — 88

49. John Marshall. Oil on canvas attributed to John Blennerhassett Martin, *ca.* 1834, 30 by 25 inches. Courtesy of William L. Marbury, Baltimore. — 89

50. John Marshall. Oil on canvas, copy or replica of figure 48 or 49, artist and date unknown, 30¼ by 25 inches. Courtesy of Washington University, St. Louis, Mo. — 90

51. John Marshall. Oil on canvas, artist and date unknown but attributed to John Blennerhassett Martin, size unknown. Owner unknown. Photograph courtesy of the Frick Art Reference Library, New York City. — 91

52. John Marshall. Engraving by Alonzo Chappel after an unlocated portrait that was one of the John Blennerhassett Martin likenesses, *ca.* 1863, 7½ by 5½ inches. Courtesy of the Massachusetts Historical Society, Boston. — 91

53. John Marshall. Wax bas-relief by Beverley Waugh, *ca.* 1830, approximately 6 inches high. Courtesy of the Virginia Historical Society, Richmond. — 94

54. John Marshall. Wax bas-relief by Beverley Waugh, *ca.* 1830, approximately 12 inches high. Courtesy of Miss Rebecca Snowden Marshall, Baltimore. — 95

55. John Marshall. Wax bust by Robert Ball Hughes, 1829, 8 inches high. Courtesy of the Supreme Court of the United States, Washington, D.C. — 97

56. John Marshall. Oil on canvas by Robert Matthew Sully, 1829, 43 by 32½ inches. Courtesy of the Richmond City Council, Old City Hall, Richmond. — 102

57. John Marshall. Ink and pencil on paper by Robert Matthew Sully, 1829, 12 by 7¾ inches. Courtesy of Victor Spark, New York City. — 105

58. John Marshall. Oil on canvas, replica perhaps after figure 56, by Robert Matthew Sully, 1855, 36 by 29 inches. Courtesy of the State Historical Society of Wisconsin, Madison. — 107

59. John Marshall. Oil on canvas by Robert Matthew Sully, 1830, 37 by 29¼ inches. Courtesy of the Corcoran Gallery of Art, Washington, D.C. — 109

60. John Marshall. Oil on canvas, artist unknown but attributed to Robert Matthew Sully, 1829–1830, 30¼ by 25¼ inches. Courtesy of the Virginia Museum of Fine Arts, Richmond. — 110

61. The Virginia Constitutional Convention of 1829–1830. Watercolor sketch by George Catlin, 1829–1830, 21⅝ by 32⅞ inches. Courtesy of The New-York Historical Society, New York City.   116

62. Key to the Virginia Constitutional Convention of 1829–1830. Pen and ink on paper by George Catlin, 1830, 20 by 33 inches (by sight). Courtesy of The New-York Historical Society, New York City.   117

63. The Virginia Constitutional Convention of 1829–1830. Oil on a walnut panel by George Catlin, 1830, 24 by 36 inches. Courtesy of the Virginia Historical Society, Richmond.   119

64. John Marshall. Gold stamping on cover of William H. Brown, *Portrait Gallery of Distinguished American Citizens, with Biographical Sketches, and Fac-similes of Original Letters* (New York, 1931 [orig. publ. Hartford, Conn., 1845]), probably taken from figure 65, artist and date unknown, approximately 5 inches high. Courtesy of The New-York Historical Society, New York City.   122

65. John Marshall. Pen and ink silhouette on paper by William H. Brown, *ca.* 1831, approximately 4 inches high. Courtesy of the Massachusetts Historical Society, Boston.   123

66. John Marshall. Pen and ink silhouette on paper by William H. Brown, date unknown, approximately 4 inches high. Courtesy of the Massachusetts Historical Society, Boston.   124

67. John Marshall. Lithograph silhouette after original by William H. Brown, artist unknown, 1844, 13⅜ by 9⅞ inches. Courtesy of The New-York Historical Society, New York City.   126

68. John Marshall and Bishop Richard Channing Moore. Pen and ink silhouette on paper, that of Marshall by or after William H. Brown, date unknown, 11¼ by 12⅞ inches. Courtesy of the Virginia Historical Society, Richmond.   127

69. John Marshall. Pen and ink silhouette on paper by William H. Brown, 1830, 13 by 10 inches. Courtesy of the Virginia Historical Society, Richmond.   128

70. John Marshall. Pen and ink silhouette on paper, probably after figure 67, by Auguste Edouart, *ca.* 1840, approximately 6½ inches tall. Courtesy of a private collector.   130

71. John Marshall. Monumental bronze statue, after figure 65 or one of its derivatives, by William Wetmore Story, 1882–1884, larger than life-size. Courtesy of the Library of Congress, Washington, D.C.   131

72. John Marshall. Bronze statue, replica of figure 71, by William

Wetmore Story, larger than life-size. Courtesy of the Commissioners of Fairmount Park, Philadelphia. 132

73. John Marshall. Oil on canvas by Henry Inman, 1831, 36 by 29 inches. Courtesy of the Philadelphia Bar Association, on loan to the Department of State, Washington, D.C. 135

74. John Marshall. Oil on canvas, replica of figure 73, by Henry Inman, 1832, 36 by 28⅞ inches. Courtesy of the Virginia State Library, Richmond. 140

75. John Marshall. Stipple and line engraving, after figure 73, by Asher B. Durand, 1833, 4⁵⁄₁₆ by 3¾ inches. Courtesy of The New-York Historical Society, New York City. 142

76. John Marshall. Oil on canvas, after figure 73, by Jacob Eichholtz, 1841, 36 by 28¼ inches. Courtesy of the Historical Society of Pennsylvania, Philadelphia. 142

77. John Marshall. Oil on canvas, after figure 73, by Jacob Eichholtz, *ca.* 1841, 30 by 25 inches. Courtesy of The Brook, New York City. 143

78. John Marshall. Oil on academy board, copy of figure 77, by William B. Chambers, date unknown, 9⅞ by 7⅜ inches. Courtesy of the New York State Office of Parks and Recreation, Taconic State Park and Recreation Commission, Philipse Manor State Historic Site. 143

79. John Marshall. Oil on canvas, after figure 73 or one of its derivatives, artist and date unknown. Courtesy of the Connecticut State Library, Hartford. 145

80. John Marshall. Engraving, after figure 79, by Charles Schlect, before 1890, 2¼ inches high. Courtesy of the Treasury Department, Bureau of Engraving and Printing, Washington, D.C. 145

81. John Marshall. Oil on canvas, probably after figure 74, artist and date unknown, 35⅜ by 28⅝ inches. Courtesy of the United States District Court for the Eastern District of Virginia, Richmond. 145

82. John Marshall. Oil on canvas, after figure 74 or one of its derivatives, artist and date unknown, 36½ by 29½ inches. Courtesy of the John Marshall Hotel, Richmond. 145

83. John Marshall. Key tag set in lucite, likeness taken from figure 82, artist unknown, 2¾ inches in diameter. Courtesy of Andrew Oliver, Boston, Mass. 147

84. John Marshall. Oil on canvas, after figure 74, by Mrs. Jeffrey G. A. Montague, 1915, 35 by 28 inches. Courtesy of the Association for the Preservation of Virginia Antiquities, John Marshall House, Richmond. 148

85. John Marshall. Oil on canvas, probably after figure 74, by John D. Slavin, 1932, 29 by 36¼ inches. Courtesy of Mrs. Kenneth R. Higgins, Richmond.   148

86. John Marshall. Oil on canvas, probably after figure 73, by William Barksdale Meyers, 1857, 37 by 30 inches. Courtesy of the Virginia Historical Society, Richmond.   148

87. John Marshall. Oil on canvas, after figure 73, by George Peter Alexander Healy, *ca.* 1845. Courtesy of Caisse Nationale des Monuments Historiques, Paris.   148

88. John Marshall. Oil on canvas, copy after figure 73 or one of its derivatives, by George C. Lambdin, *ca.* 1867, 35¾ by 29 inches. Courtesy of the Maryland Historical Society, Baltimore.   150

89. John Marshall. Oil on canvas, after figure 73, by James Reid Lambdin, 1867, 36 by 29 inches. Courtesy of the Union League of Philadelphia.   150

90. John Marshall. Oil on canvas, probably after figure 73, attributed to James Reid Lambdin, date unknown, 36 by 28 inches. Courtesy of the National Portrait Gallery, Washington, D.C.   150

91. John Marshall. Oil on canvas, after figure 73 or one of its derivatives, artist unknown, *ca.* 1840, 52 by 32 inches. Courtesy of the Stanford University School of Law, Stanford, Calif.   150

92. John Marshall. Oil on canvas, after figure 73 or one of its derivatives, artist unknown, *ca.* 1840, 30 by 24 inches. Courtesy of The College of William and Mary, Williamsburg, Va.   153

93. John Marshall. Oil on canvas, after figure 73 or one of its derivatives, by George H. Knapp, 1899, 38 by 34 inches. Courtesy of Independence National Historical Park, Philadelphia.   153

94. John Marshall. Oil on canvas, after figure 73 or one of its derivatives, artist and date unknown, 36 by 29 inches. Courtesy of the Pennsylvania Academy of the Fine Arts, Philadelphia.   153

95. John Marshall. Oil on canvas, after figure 73, by Eliphalet F. Andrews, 1891, 29½ by 24¼ inches. Courtesy of the Diplomatic Reception Rooms, Department of State, Washington, D.C.   153

96. John Marshall. Woodcut, after figure 73, artist unknown, *ca.* 1839, 3 by 3 inches. Courtesy of the Massachusetts Historical Society, Boston.   156

97. John Marshall. Wood engraving, after figure 73, by John W. Orr, 1853, 5 by 4 inches. Courtesy of The New-York Historical Society, New York City.   156

98. John Marshall. Stipple and line engraving, after figure 73 or one of its derivatives, by William G. Jackman, *ca.* 1857, 5 by 4 inches. Courtesy of The New-York Historical Society, New York City.   157

99. John Marshall. Stipple engraving, after figure 73, by Thomas B. Welch, *ca.* 1836, approximately 2 inches high. Courtesy of the National Portrait Gallery, Washington, D.C.   157

100. John Marshall. Etching, aquatint, and drypoint, after figure 73 or one of its derivatives, by Thomas Blakeman, 1935, 12 by 9¾ inches. Courtesy of S. Douglas Fleet, Richmond.   157

101. John Marshall and others. Engraved vignettes, that of Marshall after a derivative of figure 73, by John Rogers, date unknown, 8¾ by 5¾ inches. Courtesy of Herbert A. Johnson, Williamsburg, Va.   159

102. John Marshall. Oil on canvas, derived from figure 73, by William D. Washington, 1859, 109 by 63 inches. Courtesy of the Circuit Court of Fauquier County, Warrenton, Va.   160

103. John Marshall. Oil on canvas, after figure 102, by Richard N. Brooke, 1881, approximately 108 by 62 inches. Courtesy of the Library of Congress.   161

104. John Marshall. Oil on canvas, after figure 102, by David Silvette, 1946, approximately 96 by 60 inches. Courtesy of the University of Virginia, Charlottesville.   162

105. John Marshall. Oil on canvas by William James Hubard, *ca.* 1834, 20½ by 14 inches. Courtesy of the Association for the Preservation of Virginia Antiquities, John Marshall House, Richmond.   166

106. John Marshall. Oil on canvas by William James Hubard, *ca.* 1834, 21 by 15⅛ inches. Courtesy of the University of Virginia, Charlottesville.   167

107. John Marshall. Oil on canvas by William James Hubard, *ca.* 1834, 21 by 17 inches. Courtesy of Victor Spark, New York City.   167

108. John Marshall. Oil on canvas by William James Hubard, *ca.* 1834, 21¼ by 15 inches. Courtesy of the National Portrait Gallery, Washington, D.C.   168

109. John Marshall. Oil on canvas by William James Hubard, *ca.* 1834, 35¾ by 27¼ inches. Courtesy of the Association for the Preservation of Virginia Antiquities, John Marshall House, Richmond.   170

110. John Marshall. Oil on canvas by William James Hubard, *ca.* 1834, 21¼ by 15 inches. Courtesy of the Virginia Historical Society, Richmond.   170

111. John Marshall. Marble bust by John Frazee, 1834, 33 inches high. Courtesy of the Boston Athenaeum.   176

112. John Marshall. Plaster bust, after figure 111, by John Frazee, after 1834, 32¾ inches high. Courtesy of The New-York Historical Society, New York City.   177

113. John Marshall. Oil on canvas, possibly after figure 25, artist and date unknown, 29 by 24½ inches. Courtesy of the Virginia Historical Society, Richmond.   181

114. John Marshall. Marble bust by Hiram Powers, 1836, 27 inches high to the top of a 5-inch plinth. Courtesy of the Library of Congress.   182

115. John Marshall. Monumental bronze statue, as part of the Washington Monument in Richmond, by Randolph Rogers, after 1860, larger than life-size. Photograph by Dementi Studio, Inc., Richmond.   184

116. John Marshall. Stipple engraving by J. A. O'Neill, 1874, 4 by 3½ inches. From James A. Goode, *Proceedings of the M. W. Grand Lodge of Ancient York Masons of the State of Virginia, from Its Organization in 1778 to 1822* . . . (Richmond, 1874), I.   186

117. John Marshall. Oil on canvas, after figures 1 and 116, by David Silvette, 1954, 30 by 24 inches. Courtesy of The Most Worshipful Grand Lodge of Ancient, Free and Accepted Masons of the Commonwealth of Virginia, Richmond.   187

118. John Marshall. Marble bust by Hugh Cannon, 1840, 27½ inches high. Courtesy of the Philadelphia Bar Association.   188

119. John Marshall. Bronze statue by Bryant Baker, 1959, 6 feet 3 inches high. Courtesy of the Board of Supervisors of Fauquier County, Warrenton, Va.   189

120. John Marshall. Engraved reproduction of the first seal of Marshall College, artist and size unknown.   190

121. John Marshall and Benjamin Franklin. Engraved reproduction of the first seal of Franklin and Marshall College, artist and size unknown.   190

122. John Marshall and Benjamin Franklin. Seal presently in use by Franklin and Marshall College, 2 inches in diameter. Courtesy of Franklin and Marshall College, Lancaster, Pa.   190

123. John Marshall and George Wythe. Bronze medallion, designed for presentation to the Marshall-Wythe School of Law, by Carl A. Roseberg, 1962, 2¾ inches in diameter. Courtesy of the Marshall-Wythe School of Law, The College of William and Mary, Williamsburg, Va.   190

Acknowledgments

A search for portraits, busts, silhouettes, or other forms of likenesses, such as was needed to make this volume possible, necessarily places the author under obligation to many institutions and individuals. No such task could be undertaken without the aid so willingly offered by the Frick Art Reference Library and the National Portrait Gallery. The New-York Historical Society, Boston Athenaeum, Harvard Law School, American Antiquarian Society, Massachusetts Historical Society, and Alderman Library at the University of Virginia contributed generously from their resources. Members of the Marshall family have, with but a few exceptions, responded freely to inquiries and provided photographs of their holdings. Specific acknowledgment of ownership is made in the list of Illustrations. It is a privilege to record special thanks to Mrs. Kenneth R. Higgins, one of the chief justice's descendants, and to Herbert A. Johnson and Charles T. Cullen, editors of *The Papers of John Marshall*, who have all been generous of their time and special knowledge. The Association for the Preservation of Virginia Antiquities, as administrator and custodian of the John Marshall House in Richmond, has granted free access to its lode of Marshall lore. Thanks are due to all those who have granted permission to reproduce their portraits and who in many instances have gone to great pains to see that adequate prints were made available.

A personal word of appreciation is owing to the many individuals who have given assistance and encouragement: Richard I. Bonsal, D. Spencer Byard, Roger E. Comley, Clement E. Conger, Frances Davenport, Ulysse Desportes, Robert Bruce Graham, Jr., James Gregory, James J. Heslin, Catherine Hetos, Eugenia Calvert Holland, K. Conover Hunt, John Melville Jennings, Barbara A. Johnson, David B. Lawall, David McKibbin, Robert L. McNeil, Jr., Lilian M. C. Randall, Richard H. Randall, Jr., E. P. Richardson, Stephen T. Riley, E. Robert Seaver, Nicholas B. Wainwright, and Maxwell Whiteman.

The typing of the manuscript from its earliest stages was competently done by Eunice E. Viles and my daughter Ruth F. O. Morley, and my wife, as always, listened willingly and critically as the text was read aloud, matching in every respect, as she always has, Marshall's own "dearest Polly."

The Portraits of

John Marshall

Introduction

THE DESIRE to know what a particular historical figure looked like, to "see the great Achilles, whom we knew," has long been strong in the minds of inquiring historians or students of human nature. For the years before the invention of the camera—before the advent in 1839 of Louis Jacques Mandé Daguerre's famous black box—we are of necessity thrown back on portraits, on canvas or in marble, as the only answer to our longing for a likeness. Portraiture as an art has existed from time immemorial; the sands of Egypt and the villas of Pompeii produced likenesses, some of known historical persons, many perhaps only passing resemblances to "some mute inglorious Milton" resting we know not where. But the longing to see our man, to look into his face at the time he spoke or wrote the words that may have become part of our very history, is ever strong.

Art historians have responded to our need in various ways. We have been favored with so-called definitive treatises on all the portraits by this or another artist of significance. In this country, for example, we have the last word (at the date of publication) on the works of Smibert, Feke, Copley, Stuart, Charles Willson Peale, Trumbull, Greenough, and Jarvis.[1] These show us within their limits the genius of a particular artist and sometimes, too, his representation of the man we seek. Yet these few volumes, and they are few when we consider how wide the field is, only scratch the surface of the deep lode of portraiture from eighteenth- and nineteenth-century America.

1. Henry Wilder Foote, *John Smibert, Painter* . . . (Cambridge, Mass., 1950); Henry Wilder Foote, *Robert Feke: Colonial Portrait Painter* (Cambridge, Mass., 1930); Jules David Prown, *John Singleton Copley* (Cambridge, Mass., 1966); Lawrence Park, comp., *Gilbert Stuart: An Illustrated Descriptive List of His Works* . . . (New York, 1926); Charles Coleman Sellers, *Charles Willson Peale* (New York, 1969); Theodore Sizer, *The Works of Colonel John Trumbull, Artist of the American Revolution*, rev. ed. (New Haven, Conn., 1967); Nathalia Wright, *Horatio Greenough: The First American Sculptor* (Philadelphia, 1963); and Harold E. Dickson, *John Wesley Jarvis: American Painter, 1780–1840, with a Checklist of His Works* (New York, 1949).

In recent years, more particularly in the last two decades, a new approach to this aspect of portraiture has arisen, both in this country and to a lesser degree in England. During this period more than a dozen books have been published dealing not with the works of one artist but with all the known portraits of one man.[2] So now we can see John Keats as he was when he first looked into Chapman's Homer and as he was, some years later, when he lay on his deathbed and looked into eternity. We see Arthur Wellesley as a charming lad of eleven and again as he appeared as the first duke of Wellington, the hero of the Battle of Talavera. We can look at John Quincy Adams, a youth of sixteen years, as his father's secretary in The Hague and sixty years later as the "Old Man Eloquent," the champion of the right of petition. We see Aaron Burr as Jefferson's vice-president in 1802, and again thirty years later we see the adventurer as an old man a year or two before he died. Thomas Jefferson and John Adams we meet in Paris and London as the representatives of the new Republic in 1785 and forty years later as John H. I. Browere preserved them in plaster shortly before their deaths on the fiftieth anniversary of the Declaration of Independence.

John Marshall was well known to Jefferson and Adams, to Jefferson as a man with whom he strongly disagreed, to Adams as one whom he admired and trusted. Our understanding of Jefferson and Adams has been broadened by familiarity with their appearances throughout their lives as revealed in the volumes on their portraits, and it is the purpose of this volume to

2. John E. Stillwell, *The History of the Burr Portraits* (New York? 1928); John Hill Morgan and Mantle Fielding, *The Life Portraits of Washington and Their Replicas* (Philadelphia, 1931); Lord Gerald Wellesley and John Steegman, *The Iconography of the First Duke of Wellington* (London, 1935); Donald Parson, *Portraits of Keats* (Cleveland, Ohio, 1954); Frances Blanshard, *Portraits of Wordsworth* (Ithaca, N.Y., 1959); John Rupert Martin, *The Portrait of John Milton at Princeton, and Its Place in Milton Iconography* (Princeton, N.J., 1961); Charles Coleman Sellers, *Benjamin Franklin in Portraiture* (New Haven, Conn., 1962); Alfred L. Bush, *The Life Portraits of Thomas Jefferson* (Charlottesville, Va., 1962); Stanley Morison, *The Likeness of Thomas More: An Iconographical Survey of Three Centuries,* ed. Nicolas Barker (New York, 1963); William Kurtz Wimsatt, *The Portraits of Alexander Pope* (New Haven, Conn., 1965); Andrew Oliver, *Portraits of John and Abigail Adams* (Cambridge, Mass., 1967); C. Kingsley Adams and W. S. Lewis, "The Portraits of Horace Walpole," *The Walpole Society,* XLII (1969), 1–34; Andrew Oliver, *Portraits of John Quincy Adams and His Wife* (Cambridge, Mass., 1970).

disclose so far as possible the likenesses of John Marshall, the great chief justice.

Marshall has been known to most of us chiefly from the portrait painted of him by Henry Inman in 1831, a few years before he died; yet likenesses are known as far back as 1797, when he was only forty-two years old. Most of his early life was spent in Virginia, where he became an able and distinguished lawyer, active in the affairs of the Commonwealth. His appointment as minister to France and as John Adams's secretary of state in 1800 put him in the forefront as someone to be reckoned with and therefore a likely subject to be painted or modeled. The step up to chief justice of the United States in 1801 completed his ascent and insured an increasing number of likenesses.

Two likenesses of Marshall date from his year in France, and more than a score of artists depicted him as chief justice. This in itself is not at all surprising. What is unusual, however, is the remarkable number of duplicate portraits painted by many of these artists. Marshall had five sons and a daughter; Inman painted a replica of his great 1831 portrait for Marshall's daughter; John Wesley Jarvis and William James Hubard made replicas of their portraits of Marshall for all five of his sons; four or five examples (replicas or copies) are known of the portraits by Cephas Thompson, John Blennerhassett Martin, Beverley Waugh, Robert Ball Hughes, Robert M. Sully, and John Frazee. No other sitter comes to mind of whom such a duplication of portraits exists. And then in so many instances as almost to establish a pattern, we find records of Marshall family members, a son, or grandson, or a great-grandson, referring to one or another particular portrait of the justice as being by family tradition "the best likeness ever taken of him."

In trying to establish the canon of Marshall's iconography the problem has been not a scarcity of portraits but rather the great number of them, what might be characterized as families of them, spread throughout Marshall's descendants as well as in obvious public places, museums, bar associations, law schools, and courthouses. In addition to those mentioned or illustrated below there are undoubtedly many that have eluded discovery. In a few instances original portraits, or copies or replicas of originals that are known to have been painted, have dropped from sight. The likelihood, indeed the hope, is that the publication of this volume will prompt owners of Marshall portraits, busts, or silhouettes to make known their existence to the editors of *The Papers of John Mar-*

shall, Institute of Early American History and Culture, Williamsburg, Virginia, so that the record may become as complete as possible.

Chief Justice Marshall, a great figure in his own time and perhaps even more revered now, did not enjoy the popular veneration that was accorded the early presidents. One of the motives for painting portraits in the eighteenth and early nineteenth centuries in this country was to have a likeness from which to make engravings that, in turn, might be sold in quantity and thus become a source of income to both the artist and the engraver. Several portraits of the two Adams presidents were painted solely for this purpose.[3] Except in one or two instances (which resulted in commercial failure), this was not the case with Marshall's portraits. They seem to have been either painted for him or commissioned for someone else, and if Marshall liked the result he would often order replicas or copies for his children. This is why we discover so many examples of the same likeness, stemming from the same original, and also why we are faced with the difficulty, and often the impossibility, of determining which is the original portrait and which the copy or replica. Because of this lack of public demand, there are not a great many early engravings of Marshall. The most significant ones are mentioned or illustrated below, but they are few compared to those of the Adamses, Washington, or Jefferson.

It was perhaps a combination of chance and geography that determined who would paint Marshall. He missed John Singleton Copley, who left America in 1774. Gilbert Stuart, Charles Willson Peale, Edward Savage, John Trumbull, James Sharples, John H. I. Browere, Thomas Sully, and Charles Bird King each produced likenesses of one or more of the prominent figures at the turn of the century who lived in or passed through Philadelphia or Washington, yet they all overlooked Marshall. But he was caught by Fevret de Saint-Mémin, by Cephas Thompson during his sojourn in Virginia, and by George Catlin, Robert M. Sully, and Chester Harding at the "last meeting of the giants," as the Virginia Constitutional Convention of 1829–1830 was called. John Wesley Jarvis provided us with a bumper crop, as did Hubard, Frazee, and Martin, and Inman painted the likeness by which Marshall is best known.

3. Oliver, *Portraits of John and Abigail Adams*, 29, 62–65; Oliver, *Portraits of John Quincy Adams*, 74–76.

Marshall did not live into the age of the daguerreotype. We have, therefore, no mirror image by which to test the metal of his many portraits. But Saint-Mémin's physiognotrace, mechanically produced, serves as a sort of standard, and most of the painted portraits stand up to it. There are, as would be expected, some "sports," but at the same time there is a remarkable consistency in the several types of his portraits, the only difference being due, undoubtedly, not so much to Marshall's change in appearance as he grew older but rather to the eye of the artist. Hubard, Frazee, and Harding all show him as the same man, and there is no difficulty in discovering in Inman's aged chief justice the young and handsome envoy to France as he appeared in 1797. Jefferson and the two Adamses grew old, old and tired, tired and worried looking. Marshall, aged eighty, in the face of the dreaded operation for the stone only a day or two later, looks down on us from Inman's canvas as serene, as gentle and yet as firm, as he appeared before his elevation to the Court thirty years before and as he looked while on the bench throughout his career as chief justice.

It is perhaps that very consistency in his appearance, almost unscarred by the ravages of time, that supports so eloquently the consistency of his careful, measured, and reasoned interpretation and construction of the Constitution—that indeed contributed to his becoming, as he is now still remembered, the great chief justice of the United States.

Chapter 1

Earliest Likenesses

ON MAY 31, 1797, John Adams, having only recently succeeded Washington as president of the United States, nominated John Marshall, Charles Cotesworth Pinckney, and Francis Dana as envoys extraordinary and ministers plenipotentiary to France. Dana declined to serve, and Adams chose Elbridge Gerry in his place. Marshall set sail from Philadelphia on July 17. Adams said of him that he was "a plain man, very sensible, cautious, guarded, and learned in the law of nations."[1] In France the envoys became involved in the XYZ affair, and Marshall took the measure of the scheming Talleyrand. He returned home, arriving in New York on June 17, 1798, and received a warm welcome from the American people, public dinners given by members of both houses of the Congress, and a hero's welcome in Virginia, somewhat to Jefferson's chagrin.

By 1797, at only forty-three years of age, Marshall had become a distinguished and successful lawyer, had been a member of Virginia's General Assembly, and had played an important part in the Virginia ratifying convention of 1788. On January 5, 1783, he had married Mary Willis Ambler, whose father, Jaquelin Ambler, was then treasurer of Virginia.

The earliest known likeness of Marshall is a miniature said to have been painted in France in 1797 (fig. 1). It is readily recognizable as a likeness of Marshall when compared with his later portraits. The dark almond-shaped eyes, the straight tight mouth, and the kindly expression accord well with the man we later come to know as the chief justice. Just when the miniature was painted is not known, but it may have been about the time of the modeling of the small terra-cotta bust long thought to have been done by Houdon (fig. 4). The miniature was probably sent home by Marshall to his wife, who, when her husband left, could not have imagined how long his task in France would last. It was during his absence, on January 15, 1798, that his son John was born in

1. Adams to Elbridge Gerry, July 17, 1797, Charles Francis Adams, ed., *The Works of John Adams, Second President of the United States* . . . , VIII (Boston, 1853), 549.

1. John Marshall. Miniature in oil by an unknown artist, *ca.* 1797. (See also frontispiece)

2. Mary Willis Marshall (Mrs. John Marshall). Pastel by an unknown artist, 1799. (See also frontispiece)

Richmond. In August 1798, just returned from Paris, Marshall wrote to his wife, who was absent from Richmond at the time: "My dearest Polly: Poor little John is cuting teeth & of course is sick. He appeard to know me as soon as he saw me. He woud not come to me but he kept his eye fixed on me as on a person he had some imperfect recollection of. I expect he has been taught to look at the picture & had some confusd idea of a likeness." [2] No other painting of Marshall of this date is known, and we are perhaps entitled to conclude that Marshall was referring to this one and crediting his eight-month-old son with an unlikely ability to compare his father with the small picture. It is about 2½ by 2 inches in size, is set in a thin brass frame, and is owned by Mrs. Benjamin T. Woodruff of Charleston, West Virginia. This miniature was reproduced in color as the frontispiece to the first volume of Beveridge's *Life of John Marshall.*[3] The likeness is a splendid one with which to begin our iconographic study of the man.

At the same time we are able to see his "dearest Polly" in a contemporary portrait (fig. 2), a pastel, on the reverse of which is written in an eighteenth-century hand, so far unidentified,

2. Aug. 18, 1798, Marshall Papers, Swem Library, College of William and Mary, Williamsburg, Va.

3. Albert J. Beveridge, *The Life of John Marshall* (Boston, 1916–1919).

3. Mary Willis Marshall. Miniature in oil
by an unknown artist, about 1785–1790

"Mary Ambler Marshall / 1799 Richmond, Va." The likeness is
full of charm and was undoubtedly the image of his "dearest
Polly" that Marshall carried with him in his mind's eye through
their half-century together. It now belongs to William E. Wiltshire III, of Richmond, who procured it from a dealer in Connecticut. Its provenance is not known. The Empire-style dress
and the natural, unpowdered hair accord well with the date on
the portrait, but the artist's name has so far eluded discovery.

An earlier and less appealing small portrait long believed to be
of Polly was, according to tradition, painted in the late 1780s
(fig. 3), and the dress and powdered hair support the traditional
date. It is a locket miniature that belonged to Mrs. Oswald
Garrison Villard, a descendant of Marshall's sister Mary, who had
married their cousin Humphrey Marshall in 1780 and moved to
Kentucky shortly thereafter. Family tradition tells us that the
picture was sent by Marshall to his sister not long after his marriage so that the Kentucky members of the family could see his
beloved Polly. It was reproduced in the Valentine Museum's
catalog, *Richmond Portraits in an Exhibition of Makers of Richmond, 1737–1860* (Richmond, 1949), 117, and some question
was there raised about the identity of the sitter because of the
similarity to another portrait illustrated on the same page. But
the family have clung to the belief that it is indeed a likeness of
Polly.

Chapter 2

The So-Called Houdon Bust

TO AMERICAN ART HISTORIANS the name of Jean Antoine Houdon is a byword. The few busts he modeled of great Americans would alone have made his reputation in this country, though it rests more heavily on the likenesses of the multitude of famous Europeans who sat to him. The busts and statues of the few Americans he is known to have modeled are convincing and impressive likenesses.

Houdon was brought to this country, largely through the efforts of Benjamin Franklin and Thomas Jefferson, for the purpose of modeling a statue of George Washington. Marshall said of this statue, now standing like a classical god in the rotunda of the capitol in Richmond, Virginia, that "it represented the original as perfectly as a living man could be represented in marble,"[1] especially from the perspective of a half-front view on the right-hand side. Marshall had known and revered Washington in life and as a labor of love had written his five-volume *Life of George Washington* . . . (Philadelphia, 1804–1807). The great statue must have been a constant reminder of his old friend. Lafayette is reported to have said of it, "That is the man himself, I can almost realize he is going to move."[2] We, at the same time, can see before our eyes, through the work of Houdon's hands, Lafayette himself, Jefferson, John Paul Jones, Robert Fulton, and Joel Barlow. The thought, indeed the tradition, that we have also Houdon's bust of John Marshall is almost too good to be true— we want to believe it to be true. But we must examine the evidence and form our own opinion as to whether it is true.

Among the many representations of Marshall in the John Marshall House in Richmond is a small head, 5¾ inches high, the front half of which is mounted on a plaster plaque. It was placed on loan to the house in 1948 by its then owners, Mrs. Margaret Dandridge Williams Brown and her son John Herbert Brown. Tradition, often repeated and consequently long believed,

1. Mabel Munson Swan, *The Athenaeum Gallery, 1827–1873* (Boston, 1940), 163.
2. *Ibid.*

tells us that when in Paris as envoy to France in 1797, Marshall commissioned Houdon to model his bust, or as it is now sometimes called (in its dilapidated state), his life mask. He is said to have brought the head back to this country, where it later became the property of his sister Elizabeth (whose portrait hangs in the Marshall House), wife of Rawleigh Colston of Honeywood, Berkeley County, West Virginia. It then passed to her son Edward Colston, who had studied law in Marshall's office. When Honeywood was destroyed by fire during the Civil War, the bust was broken and the back of the head damaged, leaving only the face not seriously impaired. Major Innes Randolph of Baltimore, an art connoisseur of the mid-nineteenth century, is reported to have exclaimed when he saw the piece that it was "worth its weight in gold," and he asked to be allowed to repair it.[3] That he did, most skillfully, turning it into a sort of life mask or bas-relief (fig. 4). The line of a fracture can be seen at the base of what remains of the neck, and a crack running diagonally across the face is plainly visible. The head became the property of Alfred Brockenbrough Williams of Virginia, a great-grandnephew of Marshall's, and later was owned by his daughter Mrs. Margaret D. W. Brown.

In 1948 the head was in the keeping of Mrs. Ellen Page Smith of Baltimore, Mrs. Rawleigh Colston's great-great-granddaughter. Carrying out Mrs. Brown's wishes, she transmitted the head to the John Marshall House with a newspaper clipping and a letter reading in part as follows:

Unfortunately it is no longer a bust and the clipping tells of the sad accident which caused it to become a head, in fact, a beautiful fragment with the signature of the artist, Houdon, lost. I hope that you, at the John Marshall House, will not be disappointed in the size and what is left of the original bust. Mrs. Brown apparently did not go into details. It seems to me a very precious and exquisite small work of art. The workmanship of the artist so rare and beautiful, the face that of a great man. The fact that John Marshall told my great grandfather [Edward Colston], his nephew, that he considered it the best lightness [sic] that had been made of him adds greatly to its interest.

This precious fragment has always been our most prized family heirloom as since my grandmother's death, my mother, with whom I lived, took care of it. Although I shed some tears when it left the House I am very happy that my cousin, Mrs. Brown, carried out the

3. Notes by Margaret Dandridge Williams Brown, Jan. 20, 1948, Association for the Preservation of Virginia Antiquities, Richmond.

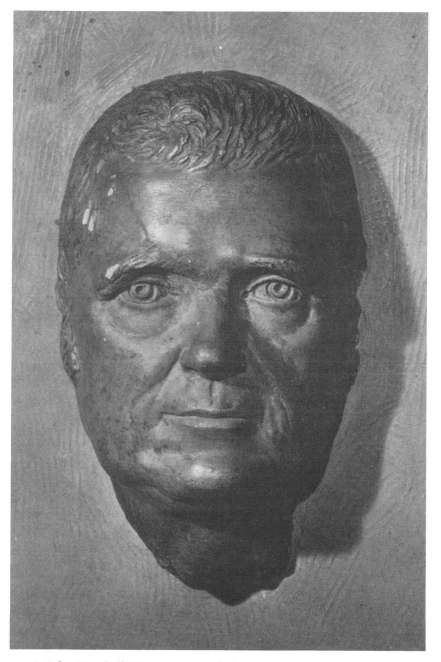

4. John Marshall. Terra-cotta mask by an unknown artist, *ca.* 1797

wishes of my mother, my sisters and myself and had the head sent to you. I hope it will always be at the John Marshall House where it certainly belongs.[4]

Mrs. Brown had apparently been encouraged to make the loan by Alexander Weddell, president of the Virginia Historical Society and an old friend of the family's. Mr. Weddell was familiar

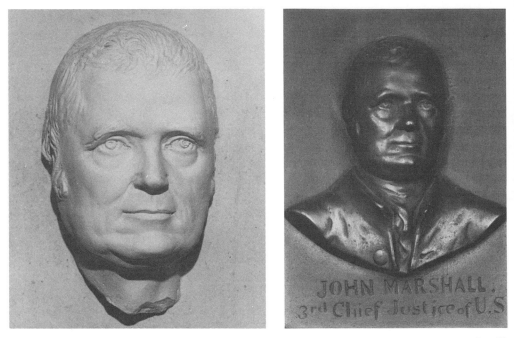

5. John Marshall. Plaster mask by an unknown artist

6. John Marshall. Plaster "metalized" bas-relief by an unknown artist

with, and undoubtedly accepted, the family tradition attributing the head to Houdon.[5]

With the tradition of its origin firmly established, it is not surprising that reproductions of the repaired head were made. One (fig. 5), the same size as the original, in plaster but with the

4. Ellen Page Smith to Marguerite Stuart Quarles, Jan. 11, 1948, Association for the Preservation of Virginia Antiquities.

5. Alexander W. Weddell to Gabrielle Page, president of the APVA, Dec. 26, 1947, Association for the Preservation of Virginia Antiquities; Alexander Wilbourne Weddell, *Portraiture in the Virginia Historical Society* (Richmond, 1945), 130–131.

crack across the face eliminated, was given by Major Innes Randolph to the Virginia Historical Society on December 19, 1882. Another (fig. 6), received by the Virginia Historical Society in 1917, had been modified by the addition of a stock and collar of the appropriate period and "metalized" to insure its preservation. The plaque owned by Mrs. Mary Marshall Swann (fig. 7) is probably a later reproduction of figure 6, though it is not clear how or when it came into the possession of Mrs. Swann's family. Another type of reproduction, believed to have been more numerous, though not many have come to light, is represented by the bronze plaque owned by Johns Hopkins University (fig. 8), and a similar one owned by Victor Spark of New York. Of the origin of these latter two we are no longer in the dark.

In the Walters Art Gallery in Baltimore is the manuscript diary of George A. Lucas, the Baltimore dealer and collector, who settled in Paris around 1860. For many years afterwards he bought books, paintings, and objets d'art for wealthy Baltimoreans as well as for the New York art dealer Samuel P. Avery and some of his clients, including William H. Vanderbilt and

7. John Marshall. Bronze bas-relief by
an unknown artist

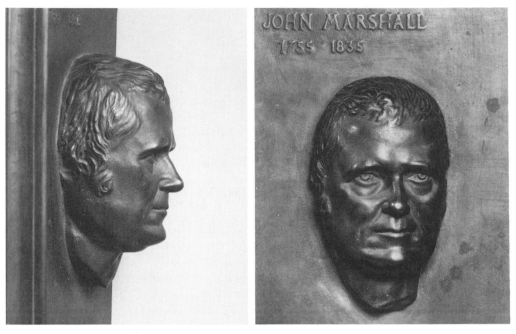

8. John Marshall. Bronze bas-relief by
Moreau Vauthier, 1890

John Taylor Johnston.[6] Lucas's diary discloses that early in 1890, in Paris, he arranged with the French sculptor Moreau Vauthier to make busts (and plaques) of Marshall, apparently to be taken from a plaster copy of the repaired original of the so-called Houdon head.[7] Lucas's diary contains some twenty-two entries on this subject between January 3, 1890, and November 30, 1891, of which the following are samples:

Jan. 3, 1890 "Ack'g receipt of Marshall to Johns Hopkins University" Mar. 10, 1890 "Sitting to Moreau for Bust—carried him the Masque of Marshall"

6. The diary of George A. Lucas was brought to my attention and the quotations from it supplied through the kindness of Lilian M. C. Randall of Baltimore. It is quoted by courtesy of the Trustees of the Walters Art Gallery, Baltimore, Md.

7. Possibly the one referred to in Anna Wells Rutledge, "Portraits in Varied Media in the Collections of the Maryland Historical Society," *Maryland Historical Magazine*, XLI (1946), 304, in which she records a "Plaster relief cast after broken bust, 11 × 8. After Jean Antoine Houdon, gift of Mrs. Alice Lee Stevenson," in 1919.

May 16, 1890 "At Moreau Vauthier to consult about casting head of Marshall"

May 19, 1890 "To consult Mr. [Daniel Coit] Gilman about bronze mask"

May 29, 1890 "Mr. Gilman left today, showed him the project for the Bronze J. Marshall, carried same to Moreau"

July 26, 1890 "At Moreau Vauthier & paid bills of Rudier & others 460 fs for Gilman bronzes"

Oct. 13, 1890 "Wrote . . . Gilman about Bronzes plaque J. Marshall & bill for same 460 fs"

May 12, 1891 "At Chaplains & had talk about making new model of John Marshall"

Oct. 24, 1891 "At Rudiers & ordered 15 Busts J. Marshall for 45 fs each"

Nov. 30, 1891 "Certified Correct to Rudiers bill of casting 15 bronze Medallions John Marshall for Mr. Gilman"

After the extensive remodeling of Gilman Hall at Johns Hopkins University, several of the Vauthier bronzes of Marshall were discovered in 1967, some mounted on oak panels, others on bronze plaques, including the one owned by Johns Hopkins (fig. 8). More are undoubtedly at large. Their reproduction of the original is faithful.

The head, in all its various forms, is clearly a likeness of Marshall; in profile it compares well with the Saint-Mémin drawing (fig. 10 and chap. 3). Its being treasured by the family is consistent with their custom of preserving and revering all of Marshall's many portraits. That this bust was thought to be by Houdon undoubtedly increased its interest, but except for tradition there is no evidence that he modeled it.

Most of Houdon's subjects were very prominent persons at the time he modeled their busts. In his 1918 study of Houdon, Georges Giacometti listed only six American sitters—Washington, Jefferson, Franklin, Robert Fulton, John Paul Jones, and Joel Barlow—some of whom were the subjects of several busts or statues by Houdon.[8] In a later revision Giacometti wrote that to his knowledge the sole production of sculpture by Houdon in 1797 and 1798 was a medallion in terra-cotta formerly in the collection of Jacques Domet and sold when the collection was dispersed in 1912; Giacometti had encountered no other works

8. Georges Giacometti, *Le Statuaire Jean-Antoine Houdon et son epoque* (*1741–1828*) (Paris, 1918), II, 1. Recording those by Houdon in Richmond, Giacometti includes only Washington and Lafayette. *Ibid.*, 28.

made in those years.[9] But Marshall's bust, if by Houdon, must
have been done in one of those years. That the only Americans
modeled by Houdon are the six listed above is borne out by
H. H. Arnason, the American authority on Houdon.[10]

The existing head of Marshall (fig. 4), is only 5¾ inches high.
Houdon's habit (to which there are some exceptions) was to
model busts or heads nearly if not exactly life-size. Note, for
example, Louis Boilly's painting of Houdon in his study modeling
the marquis de Laplace in 1804 while observed by his family, the
painting now owned by the Musée des Arts Décoratifs in Paris.[11]
Here we see the sculptor at work on a life-size bust, and ranged
around the room on high shelves are two score or more busts, all
approximately life-size. Why in Marshall's case would he have
made a miniature? Even more telling is the dissimilarity of this
head, as a work of art, to Houdon's style and power. It does not
meet the standard of quality we come to expect of Houdon. It
has been well said, "In the last analysis it must always be remembered that in the case of many of the great figures and
personalities of the latter 18th century, it was Houdon who cre-
ated the familiar visual image." [12] When we think of Voltaire or
Molière, Franklin or John Paul Jones, it is Houdon's portrait that
comes to mind. This could never be said of the little terra-cotta
head of Marshall at the John Marshall House. It is soft, characterless, unconvincing as a work of art though acceptable as a likeness, especially in profile, but it doesn't reveal the man we see in
Saint-Mémin's profile.

Sculptors and artists were plentiful in France in the late eighteenth century. No doubt one of them modeled Marshall while he
was there in 1797. By the time the head had passed down through
the family for several generations and had been repaired after
being partially destroyed in the 1860s, it is not hard to believe
that the true artist's name had been forgotten and that by some
chance the name of Houdon had become attached to it.

The bust of Marshall at the Hall of Fame, New York University
(fig. 9), has been said to have been taken in part from the so-
called Houdon mask, but it doesn't resemble the mask any more
than it resembles Marshall himself as we have come to know him
from all his life portraits.

9. Georges Giacometti, *La Vie et l'oeuvres de Houdon* (Paris, 1929),
I, 84.
10. H. H. Arnason, *Sculpture of Houdon* (Worcester, Mass., 1964), 13.
11. Reproduced *ibid.*, 8–9.   12. *Ibid.*, 12.

9. John Marshall. Bronze bust by
Herbert Adams, 1925

Research conducted in 1972 when further reproductions of the terra-cotta head (fig. 4) were under consideration confirms that it was not from the hand of Houdon.[13] What we have to accept, it would seem, is that it was as a "Houdon" head that the little terra-cotta mask was so often the subject of reproduction—not as an outstanding likeness of Marshall. On the latter account alone it is unlikely that anyone would have sought so often to have it reproduced.

13. The terra-cotta head was examined in 1972 by H. H. Arnason and a conservator at the Metropolitan Museum of Art, and the attribution to Houdon was rejected.

Chapter 3

Charles Balthazar Julien
Fevret de Saint-Mémin
(1770–1852)

THE PANTOGRAPH cannot lie. Profiles mechanically taken by the famous physiognotrace first introduced in this country by Charles Balthazar Julien Fevret de Saint-Mémin can only be true profiles. Saint-Mémin, the artist, however, discloses his own talent in the manner in which the mechanically produced outline profile is embellished—in black crayon on pink tinted paper. The process was invented by Gilles-Louis Chrétien in 1786; the popularity it achieved abroad instigated Saint-Mémin's bringing it to this country. Born in Dijon in 1770, he came to America and settled in Philadelphia in 1797. For some seventeen years he traveled about taking profiles. He provided the sitter with the original drawing, usually about 21 by 15 inches in size, together with an engraved plate on which was a circular image about 2 inches in diameter and twelve engravings from it, for a total price variously stated to be $20, $30, and $33.

Saint-Mémin enjoyed great popularity in America. He returned to France in 1814, where he was made curator of the Museum of Dijon, a post he held until his death in 1852 "in the bosom of the Catholic Church, in the faith of which he had lived faithful in the midst of the infidelity of the end of the eighteenth century and during a long sojourn upon a Protestant soil." [1] Collections of his little prints, exceeding 800 in one instance, are now preserved in the Corcoran Gallery of Art, the Princeton University Library, and the Pierpont Morgan Library. A volume reproducing 760 likenesses was published in 1862. [2]

Saint-Mémin had moved from Philadelphia to Baltimore in 1804; from 1805 to 1807 he was in Washington, Alexandria, and Annapolis; from 1807 to 1808 in Richmond and Norfolk; and the following two years in Charleston. The Burr trial was in progress while he was in Richmond, and he resided on Main Street oppo-

---

1. Elias Dexter, *The St.-Mémin Collection of Portraits; Consisting of Seven Hundred and Sixty Medallion Portraits, Principally of Distinguished Americans* (New York, 1862), 8.

2. *Ibid.*

site the Custom House, where he had an opportunity to take the profiles of many of the leading figures in the trial. Among his sitters was Chief Justice Marshall, whose likeness is striking and handsome and perhaps one of his most familiar portraits (fig. 10). Exactly when the profile was taken is not known, and there are conflicting theories. The label now appearing on the original at Duke University states that it was made in 1801, which is believed to be incorrect. It was reproduced as the frontispiece to the first volume of John F. Dillon's *John Marshall*, where the illustration is stated to have been taken from the original done in March 1808.[3] The Burr trial took place during the summer and fall of 1807, and the drawing has, by another tradition, been dated in 1807. Some date in late 1807 or early 1808 would probably be most correct.

The original drawing (fig. 10) descended to one of Marshall's granddaughters, Margaret Marshall, who married her cousin Thomas Marshall Smith. Their son, bearing his father's name, carried on a correspondence about the drawing with Professor James B. Thayer of the Harvard Law School in 1900 and 1901. Professor Thayer, then at work on his memorial of Marshall for the centennial observance of his appointment as chief justice, was trying to discover all known likenesses of Marshall. Smith opened the correspondence with a letter to Professor Thayer's son, Dr. William S. Thayer, in which he says he would welcome a visit from Dr. Thayer and his father. Of the Saint-Mémin drawing he added: "The Judges of the Supreme Court at Washington, thought so highly of it, that I consented to let them have it copied as they wished to have it hung in the Court Room." [4] Smith then referred Professor Thayer to an article by Justice Joseph P. Bradley that had appeared in the *Century* magazine in 1889. Bradley's article gives an account of Saint-Mémin and his profile of Marshall and dates it in March 1808, adding that the cost for the original and twelve engraved copies was said to have been $33. Bradley also wrote that Smith had allowed the original to be photographed by "Rice of Washington" for the Supreme Court, reserving the copyright. The article is accompanied by an engraving from Rice's photograph, which at the time was believed to be the only engraved reproduction of that likeness. It

3. John F. Dillon, comp. and ed., *John Marshall: Life, Character and Judicial Services* . . . (Chicago, 1903).

4. Thomas M. Smith to W. S. Thayer, Nov. 2, 1900, Thayer Papers, Harvard University Law School, Cambridge, Mass.

10. John Marshall. Physiognotrace by C. B. J. Fevret de Saint-Mémin, 1808

bears the inscription "Engraved by J. H. E. Whitney after a crayon drawing by Saint Memin–copyright, 1889, by Thomas Marshall Smith." [5]

Smith wanted to give Thayer a copy of his drawing but did not have one left; "I shall see," he wrote, "what can be done towards having some copies made." [6] A few days later he wrote that he had ordered a print from a negative in his possession (presumably the negative made by Rice) but that it was a disappointing failure. The cost of a new negative was inescapable if copies were to be had. He concluded, "As it is, to have a copy made like the one given to the Supreme Court of the U.S., it will cost what the negative did then, about One Hundred Dollars. Unfortunately I cannot afford this expense myself, or it would give me the greatest pleasure to give every one a copy who wished it. If you think your law class can appropriate the above amount I will have the work done at once and under my direction." [7] This letter bears a somewhat illegible notation in Thayer's hand that seems to indicate he authorized Smith to proceed, which he did with expedition. Smith must have had copies made immediately and apparently gave some away. He wrote to Thayer:

I found your letter of the 16th upon my return to the City and hasten to answer it. I had no idea that the Harvard Law School would object to my letting others have copies of the St. Memin portrait, when I accepted their offer. I took it for granted that they intended me to do so when they tendered me the negative after obtaining their copies. . . . The fact is, since it has become known that the St. Memin portrait is by far the best ever taken of the Chief Justice, I have had so many inquiries from different parts of the Country, that I do not see how I can longer keep it from the public, although I have endeavored for years to do so; until now it has begun to look rather selfish in me.[8]

This letter has Thayer's notation that it was answered on December 19. "You were entirely right. . . . For what price can we make full size 1st rate copies?"

In the next letter that has come to light Smith wrote: "I have allowed C. Klackner of No. 7 28 Street to make a copy of the original, and refer you to him for information on the subject.

5. Joseph P. Bradley, "Saint-Mémin's Portrait of Marshall," *Century Illustrated Monthly Magazine*, XXXVIII (May–Oct. 1889), 778–781.

6. Smith to James B. Thayer, Dec. 3, 1900, Thayer Papers.

7. Smith to J. B. Thayer, Dec. 9, 1900, *ibid*.

8. Smith to J. B. Thayer, Dec. 18, 1900, *ibid*.

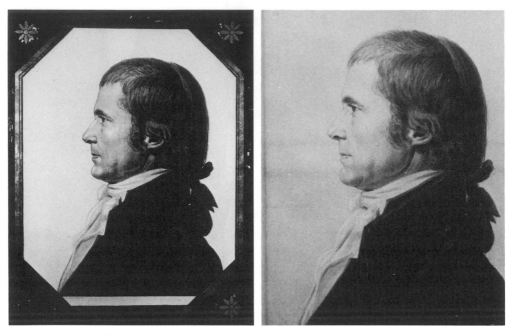

11. John Marshall. Photoengraving by   12. John Marshall. Photoengraving, 1888
    Christian Klackner, 1901

. . . A proof of his work was sent to me a few days ago, for endorsement etc., & I think he has gotten it as nearly perfect as it can well be." [9]

Professor Thayer must have written promptly to Christian Klackner, for he shortly received the following reply: "I am sending you on approval a framed copy of Chief Justice Marshall. I can supply copies in the sheet with white margin size of Engraved part 24-1/4 × 14-3/4 @ $12.00. The framed copy I am sending is like the original with exception of the frame. On the original drawing there is a Florentine frame." [10] Here this correspondence ends, but many copies of the portrait were made and distributed, bearing on the lower left-hand margin the inscription "Copyright Thos. Marshall Smith 1901." The copy now hanging in the John Marshall House in Richmond (fig. 11) is said to have been the first gift to the house after the Association for the Preservation of Virginia Antiquities was given custody of the Marshall home

9. Smith to J. B. Thayer, Jan. 7, 1901, *ibid.*
10. Klackner to J. B. Thayer, Jan. 19, 1901, *ibid.*

in 1911. A copy owned by the Philadelphia Bar Association (fig. 12) has a letter pasted on its frame:

Washington, D.C.   Dec. 20, 1888
Saml. Dickson, Esquire
Dear Sir:
    The words to be entered for the copyright on the picture [   ] here, or margin are
    "Copyright 1888
    by T. Marshall Smith"
(See act June 18, 1874, 18 Stat. Large 78)

Yours truly
Joseph P. Bradley

The difference in the two copyright dates can be explained by remembering that the 1888 date relates to the copies made at the time that one was given to the Supreme Court, while the 1901 date pertains to the copies made during the correspondence with Professor Thayer.

At some time about 1910 Thomas Marshall Smith apparently decided to sell the original Saint-Mémin drawing. He tried unsuccessfully to interest the Supreme Court in the purchase at what is reputed to have been $30,000, which seems a high figure for that time. It was finally sold in 1932 to his cousin Walton Marshall, for "around $13,000," and acquired from him by Edward C. Marshall, who bequeathed it in 1954 to the Duke University School of Law at Durham, North Carolina. The portrait, which now hangs in a prominent place in the law school courtroom, bears the inscription on a plaque: "Chief Justice John Marshall, Chief Justice of the United States 1801–1835. Portrait by Fevret de Saint Memin 1801. Bequeathed by Edward Carrington Marshall, Charlotte, North Carolina, great-grandson of Chief Justice Marshall."

One of the small engravings made from Saint-Mémin's plate, two inches in diameter, is now owned by the Corcoran Gallery of Art (fig. 13), having been part of the set of engravings of Saint-Mémin's profiles purchased for the gallery in 1878 by William Wilson Corcoran. It appears as number 592 in Dexter's volume, *The St.-Memin Collection of Portraits*. Another belongs to Mrs. Kenneth R. Higgins of Richmond, a great-great-great-granddaughter of Marshall's. Others of the little engravings were owned by members of the Marshall family but have not been found. The frontispiece to the 1899 Standard Library Edition of Allan B. Magruder, *John Marshall*, which is a reproduction of one of these engravings, is stated to be "from a miniature by St. Mémin, in the possession of Miss Annie Harvie, of Richmond, a daughter of the only daughter of Chief Justice Marshall," and "the negative was kindly lent by Mrs. Sallie Marshall Hardy, of Louisville, Ky." [11] This was probably the miniature engraving that Ellen Harvie Wade showed to Professor Thayer in 1901 and that she referred to in a letter of that year. The only others she knew of, Wade wrote to Thayer, were the miniature on ivory (fig. 1), "such as you have often seen, when he was about thirty-five," and

13. John Marshall. Engraving by
C. B. J. Fevret de Saint-Mémin, 1808

a tiny one, "set as a breast pin, neither of which have ever been copied." [12]

In 1885 George D. Fisher of Richmond corresponded with Charles C. Soule, lawbook seller of Boston, who wished to reproduce and distribute a good likeness of Marshall. Fisher consulted his second cousin Mrs. Ellen Ruffin, a granddaughter of Marshall's, about the matter and wrote Soule that Mrs. Ruffin had "a small engraving perhaps 2 or 3 inches taken many years before his death. It is a profile but from *my* recollection of him when I was about 16 years old, to his death on the 6th of July 1835 this small engraving profile, is the most *agreeable* likeness I know of, and

11. Allan B. Magruder, *John Marshall*, in *American Statesmen*, Standard Library Edition, X (Cambridge, Mass., 1899), xiii.

12. Ellen Harvie Wade to J. B. Thayer, May 29, 1901, Harvie Papers, Virginia Historical Society, Richmond.

simply because he was a younger man by 20 to 30 years, when a
fine and excellent portrait was executed of him in Phila. by an
eminent Artist and which now hangs in the 2nd story of our Capitol. . . ." [13] Fisher sent Soule a negative of the small Saint-Mémin
engraving, and it, with the Inman likeness, was reproduced for
duplication by Soule. But at that time neither Fisher nor Mrs.
Ruffin had any recollection as to who had made the miniature profile.

14. John Marshall. Bronze medal by Karl H. Gruppe, 1965

In 1901 at the Centennial Banquet given by the Virginia State
Bar Association in memory of the chief justice, a reproduction of
the small Saint-Mémin engraving was printed at the head of the
menu, a copy of which is among the Thayer Papers at the Harvard Law School.

In the John Marshall House there is today a small and rather
crude medal about 1½ inches in diameter and of unknown origin,
though clearly taken from the Saint-Mémin likeness. On the reverse is the inscription "American Jurist / Born / Sept. 24th 1755 /
Died July 6th 1835," embellished with the scales of justice and a
laurel chaplet.

It is not at all surprising that such a striking and handsome likeness taken at such a critical time in Marshall's career should have

13. Fisher to Soule, July 17, 1885, Letters of George D. Fisher relating
to John Marshall, University of Virginia Library, Charlottesville. Fisher's
reference was to the Inman portrait, the replica of which (fig. 74) then
hung in the capitol in Richmond.

often been copied or used as a model for later representations of him. The sculptor Karl H. Gruppe used it for the medal he designed for the Hall of Fame for Great Americans at New York University in 1965 (fig. 14). Gruppe wrote, "I relied chiefly on the striking profile crayon drawing by the French artist, Fevret de Saint Memin, and the three-quarter face painting by Cephas Thompson" (fig. 15).[14] The reverse of the medal shows a female figure representing the authority of the Supreme Court. In one hand she holds the scales of justice, while the other rests on the fasces, which represents the unity of the several states preserved with equal justice under law. The medal was produced in two sizes, 3 inches in bronze and 1¾ inches in bronze and in silver.

14. Gruppe's comments were printed in a folder that accompanied the Marshall medal.

Chapter 4

Cephas Thompson
(1775–1856)

THE THIRD MEETINGHOUSE of the First Church in Middleboro, Massachusetts, was erected in 1745 on the Upper Green near the present church and stood until 1829. At the time it was the largest and most imposing structure in town. The inside of the church was surrounded with deep galleries on three sides, while opposite the pulpit was a higher gallery, reserved for Indians and slaves and always said to have been well filled. The galleries were supported by pillars, which in the church's latter days were painted in rough imitation of marble sculpture by Cephas Thompson, the celebrated local portrait painter.[1]

Thompson had been born in Middleboro in 1775, son of "Squire Bill" Thompson, and from earliest boyhood could draw excellent likenesses of his schoolmates. For many years he was a successful portraitist in the South, working in Baltimore in 1804, Richmond in 1809 and 1810, and New Orleans in 1816. After 1825 he lived in Middleboro until his death, and many a house in the old town still boasts a portrait from his brush. A friend of Parke Custis's, Jefferson's and Marshall's, Thompson used to tell that "once when in Richmond, having occasion to go into the court house when the chief-justice was presiding, he was invited to take a seat with him on the bench, and he remained there during the session of the day."[2]

When in Richmond he advertised his profession on several occasions between November 14, 1809, and February 23, 1810; for example: "C. Thompson—PORTRAIT PAINTER—Respectfully informs the inhabitants of Richmond and its vicinity, that he has commenced business, in the house opposite the Swan-Tavern—where some specimens may be seen."[3]

---

1. Thomas Weston, *History of the Town of Middleboro, Masssachusetts* (Cambridge, Mass., 1906), 452.
2. *Ibid.*, 390–391.
3. Valentine Museum, *Richmond Portraits in an Exhibition of Makers of Richmond, 1737–1860* (Richmond, 1949), 233.

It must therefore have been in the winter of 1809–1810 that he took Marshall's likeness. As in so many instances, several examples exist, and we cannot conclusively identify the original. It is believed to be the portrait now owned by Johns Hopkins University (fig. 15), which hangs in Homewood House on the university campus. This painting, oil on canvas, 27½ by 22½ inches, was presented to the university in 1954 by Mabel Brady Garvan. It had apparently been kept by the artist and was purchased from a grandchild by Mrs. M. L. Binney, who sold it to Francis P. Garvan around 1902. At that time, and according to a label once on its frame, it was attributed to Jeremiah Paul. The reason for this attribution is understandable. In 1815 an engraving of Marshall appeared in the *Port Folio* magazine, 3⅞ by 3⅛ inches in size and inscribed, "J. Paul Pinx – D. Edwin fc. / John Marshall / Chief Justice of U.S." (fig. 16).[4] David Edwin (1776–1841) was a well-known stipple engraver, born in England, who worked under Edward Savage and for many years was active in Philadelphia. Paul (d. 1820) is known as a portrait, figure, and animal painter. He was a fellow pupil with Rembrandt Peale; in 1803 he was painting miniatures and tracing profiles at Charleston, later in Baltimore, and in 1811 he exhibited his *Venus and Cupid* in Philadelphia. He turned to painting portraits and signs in Pittsburgh in 1814 and later tried his hand at theatrical scenery in the West. But no connection with Marshall appears in his known record except what is implied by the inscription on this small engraving.

We have to deal with Edwin's engraving, however, and the fact, as mentioned above, that it is inscribed as having been after a likeness that "J. Paul Pinx." The question is, then, did Paul paint Marshall from life or did he merely paint a picture (copying another artist) that Edwin could reproduce in engraving? Marshall the lawyer and judge knew well the surprises that "evidence" can present; now we are thrown back on the evidence. The first thing that is apparent – to the sophisticated observer – is that Edwin's engraving (fig. 16), seen through a mirror, is almost identical to Thompson's portrait (fig. 15). Edwin's Marshall looks to our right, while Thompson's portrait looks to our left. This is a common occurrence when an engraver hasn't troubled to engrave a reverse image (perhaps with the aid of a mirror) and offers us instead something that has about it an air of originality based on

4. *The Port Folio*, 3d Ser., V (1815), 1.

15. John Marshall. Oil by Cephas Thompson, 1809–1810

16. John Marshall. Engraving by David Edwin, 1815

nothing but the unfamiliarity of a reversed image.[5] Bearing in mind that an engraver has great leeway in the subsidiary elements of his representation, we must not be misled by the details of clothing, background, highlights, and so forth. Still, it is hardly believable that Thompson's portrait (fig. 15) and Edwin's engraving (after Paul) (fig. 16) can be independent representations. One, it seems, must derive from the other or from some common source.

We know that Thompson was in Virginia, that he knew Mar-

5. See, for example, Houston's 1797 engraving of John Adams after a portrait by Sharples, in Oliver, *Portraits of John and Abigail Adams*, 78–79.

shall, and that his likeness of Marshall has been reproduced by others but usually attributed to him. It seems inconceivable that Paul could have been the originator of this particular likeness; that would require that all the so-called Thompson portraits of Marshall were simply copies of a lost Paul original. Possible but unlikely. Paul's "lost original," engraved by Edwin, does, however, give us a date for this representation of the chief justice. Here we see Marshall shortly before 1815, sixty years old, eight years after the Burr trial.

What has been the fate of this likeness? Not inconsiderable. At some point after the years 1810 to 1815 Jane Braddock Peticolas (1791–1852) painted a similar likeness for the chief justice's friend James Brown, Sr., whose wife was her sister. It would seem that she copied the Thompson portrait of 1809–1810 now at Johns Hopkins (fig. 15). Her copy (fig. 17) descended to Brown's granddaughter, Mrs. Ann Boykin of Richmond, and was acquired in 1967 by Mrs. John M. Gatewood of Richmond. The Peticolas copy is in poor condition, but there can be little doubt that it was taken from the earlier portrait. Another version (fig. 18), now dropped from sight, was in the Van Sweringen sale of October 25 to 28, 1938, at the Parke Bernet Galleries in New York City, where, as lot 824, it fetched $290.

But that is not all. The Association of the Bar of the City of New York has a portrait (fig. 19) hanging in the Tweed Room of the association's quarters on West 43d Street, New York City, which was for some time attributed to Sully—an attribution made presumably without awareness of the Johns Hopkins portrait by Thompson or the Peticolas copy. The portrait, 27¼ by 22½ inches, was bequeathed to the bar association by the late Thomas H. Rodman in the late nineteenth century, though the association's records of the portrait are not clear. In the *Green Bag*, December 1896, it is stated that "a good likeness belongs to the Washington and Lee University [fig. 39], and a very handsome one to the Bar Association of New York. It was the gift of one of New York's prominent lawyers and hangs in their rooms." [6] Who painted the bar association picture is unknown, but it does justice to Thompson's skill.

Yet there is still another. In the John Marshall House in Richmond there hangs a similar likeness (fig. 20) by an unknown

6. *The Green Bag: An Entertaining Magazine for Lawyers,* VIII (1896), 492.

17. John Marshall. Oil by Jane Braddock Peticolas, after 1810

18. John Marshall. Oil by an
unknown artist

19. John Marshall. Oil by an
unknown artist

20. John Marshall. Oil by an
unknown artist

21. John Marshall. Oil by an
unknown artist

artist that clearly stems from Thompson. It is on loan from Charles E. A. Marshall, a great-grandson of the chief justice's, having been left to him when a minor by his father and placed in the Marshall House on loan by his mother. Nothing more is known of its history.

One more Cephas Thompson copy is known (fig. 21). In 1921 F. W. Bayley, the Boston art dealer, gave the Massachusetts Historical Society a photograph of a portrait of Marshall attributed by Bayley to Charles Willson Peale. There is no record of who owned the portrait at that time, but it later turned up in the hands of André Rueff, a Brooklyn dealer, and then in 1942 in the possession of Arthur Meeker of Chicago, who sold it to Albert H. Wiggin of New York, still attributed to Peale. The portrait dropped from sight until 1957, when it was presented by Mrs. Lynde Selden to the Yale University Art Gallery, with the Peale attribution. It is now on loan to the Bowdoin College Museum of Art. Over the years Bayley's attributions of portraits have become suspect. Whether this is the original Thompson portrait of Marshall or a replica or copy is not known, but it is clearly not a copy by Peale.

The sculptor Karl H. Gruppe, who designed the Marshall medal (fig. 14) for the Hall of Fame for Great Americans in 1965, wrote that he relied on Saint-Mémin's pantographic drawing (fig. 10) and on the "three-quarter face painting by Cephas Thompson." The medal resembles the Saint-Mémin profile, but it is hard to find the influence of Thompson's likeness.

One thing, however, seems apparent: there is sufficient evidence in the various copies or replicas to attribute the original to Cephas Thompson and not to Jeremiah Paul. Whether iconographically this fairly represents Marshall as he appeared in or about the years 1810 to 1815 is a good question, and one that is often asked when a familiar figure is portrayed by different artists. It may well be one more bit of evidence that will lead to a clearer understanding of the man. Each artist sees his sitter through his own eyes. Yet, if this were but one of three types, placed, say, between Saint-Mémin's profile (fig. 10) and Inman's great portrait (fig. 73), it would be hard to see in Thompson's characterization the man who was undoubtedly our greatest chief justice.

Chapter 5

Joseph Wood

(*ca.* 1778–1830)

HE FEBRUARY 1817 issue of the *Analectic Magazine and Naval Chronicle* contained, opposite page 89, an engraving of Marshall (fig. 22), which bore the inscription "J. Wood Pinxt.–F. Kearny Sculp. / Chief Justice Marshall. / Engraved for the Analectic Magazine, Publid. by M. Thomas. / Entered According to Act of Congress." It was placed opposite a review of Augustus B. Woodward's *Classification of the Sciences;* and in the copy that I examined there was tipped in a slip reading, "A biography of Chief Justice Marshall, whose portrait accompanies this article will be given in the course of the present volume, and the portrait can be placed opposite to it when bound." These were proper instructions to a subscriber who, at the end of the year, could bind up the several numbers of the magazine and at that time place the engraving of Marshall where it would belong. But I found no such biography.

"J. Wood" was undoubtedly the painter Joseph Wood, who specialized in cabinet-sized and miniature paintings. The son of a New York farmer, he was born in Clarkstown, New York, about 1778, and was for some years a partner in New York, both in art and in dissolute living, with John Wesley Jarvis. When the partnership broke up about 1813, after the two had "indulged in the excitements and experienced the perplexities of *mysterious marriages*,"[1] Wood moved to Philadelphia and then in 1816 to Washington, where he died in 1830. Francis Kearny, engraver and lithographer, born in Perth Amboy, New Jersey, in 1785, had served his apprenticeship under the well-known engraver Peter R. Maverick. In 1810 he moved to Philadelphia, where he lived for a score of years. The *Analectic Magazine* was published in Philadelphia, and Kearny, as an accomplished engraver, was a natural choice to engrave a portrait of Marshall. No portrait of Marshall by Wood has been found, but that he did paint one is indicated

1. William Dunlap, *History of the Rise and Progress of the Arts of Design in the United States* (Boston, 1834), II, 77. The Dover reprint (New York, 1969) retains the same pagination as the 1834 edition.

22. John Marshall. Engraving by Francis Kearny, 1817

by the following letter written by Marshall from Richmond to the publisher Joseph Delaplaine on March 22, 1818:

I received while at Washington your letters requesting me to sit for my portrait to be taken first by Mr. Wood & afterwards by Mr. Lawrence. The first gentleman I could not see & the last did not reach Washington during my stay in the city. At your request my portrait was formerly taken by Mr. Wood, & I did suppose it was in your possession. His price I presume as well as that of Mr. Lawrence is forty dollars. If it is, & you can receive from him that which he has already painted, & you direct me to remit to him or yourself, I will do so.

I have also received your letter requesting some account of my birth parentage etc. . . . It is not however my wish to appear in your next half volume, nor is it my opinion that persons who are still in the view of the public ought to be placed in it. But I do not pretend to interfere with any mode of conducting your great work which to yourself shall seem eligible. . . .

I received also a letter from you requesting some expression of my sentiments respecting your repository, & indicating an intention to publish in some conspicuous manner, the certificates which might be given by Mr. Wirt & myself.

I have been ever particularly unwilling to obtain this kind of distinction, & must insist in not receiving it now. I have however no difficulty in saying that your work is one in which the nation ought to feel an interest, & I sincerely wish it may be encouraged, & that you may receive ample compensation for your labor & expence. . . . The portraits, an objective of considerable interest are, so far as my acquaintance extends, good likenesses; & the printing is neatly executed with an excellent type. . . . But as it is, we behold in it a great national undertaking & I cordially wish it success.[2]

There is no reason to doubt, therefore, that Kearny's engraving, only 4⁵⁄₁₆ by 3⁷⁄₁₆ inches in size, is a fair reproduction of Wood's life portrait taken probably about 1816. It bears some faint resemblance to Marshall but has to be compared with other likenesses nearest to it in date, such as Cephas Thompson's portrait of 1810 (fig. 15) and Rembrandt Peale's of 1825 (fig. 28), the latter of which is closer to it in appearance. Kearny's reproduction is not a satisfactory or familiar likeness, but Wood's work was probably not an acceptable portrait to begin with.[3] Yet it is nevertheless a likeness by which Marshall must have been known in 1817, at least by the readers of the *Analectic Magazine*.

2. Marshall Papers, Library of Congress. Delaplaine's project was the publication of a multivolume work entitled *Delaplaine's Repository of the Lives and Portraits of Distinguished American Characters*, the first half volume of which was published in 1816 and the second in 1817. It was not a success, and Delaplaine had as little success with John Adams as he did with Marshall; see Oliver, *Portraits of John and Abigail Adams*, 144–146.

3. Compare Wood's portrait of John Quincy Adams in Oliver, *Portraits of John Quincy Adams*, 107 (fig. 48) for an "un-likeness" and the miniatures of President Monroe and his wife in the Virginia Historical Society, *An Occasional Bulletin*, No. 15 (Oct. 1967), 3–5.

Chapter 6

Samuel Finley Breese Morse
(1791–1872)

MORSE, the perfecter of the telegraph and the code that bears his name, was also a portrait painter, and in 1822 he painted what was perhaps his greatest picture, *The Old House of Representatives* (fig. 23). "The *Time* chosen," he wrote, "is at candle lighting while the members are assembling for an evening session."[1] In the middle background can be seen the great candelabra as it was lighted, casting its shadow and lighting up the faces of the members of the House.

The theme of the great view had been devised in late 1821, and the work was begun promptly at the turn of the year. "I have commenced today taking the likenesses of the members," Morse wrote to his wife on January 2. "I found them not only willing to sit, but apparently esteeming it an honor. . . . I find the picture is becoming the subject of conversation, and every day gives me greater encouragement."[2] Each of the eighty-six persons represented sat to him in a room near the hall, except William Lowndes, whose portrait was taken from the gallery while the House was in session. Morse worked at a feverish pace, fourteen hours a day. He would rise at daybreak and be at his easel long before the congressional day began, and throughout the day the members would visit him, two hours to a sitter. In the afternoon they would often find him with a cup of tea in one hand and a pencil in the other. He worked so rapidly that by the tenth of February he was able to leave Washington and return home, reaching New Haven in six days by stage.

He himself tells us, in a short statement published early in 1823, of his purpose in painting the House, which he described as "one of the most splendid Legislative Halls in the world": "The primary design of the present picture is not so much to give highly

1. S. F. B. Morse, *Key to Morse's Picture of the House of Representatives,* (New Haven, Conn., 1823), 4.
2. Samuel I. Prince, *The Life of Samuel F. B. Morse, LL.D.* (New York, 1875), 124.

23. The Old House of Representatives. Oil by Samuel Finley Breese Morse, 1822

24. Detail of figure 23

finished likenesses of the individuals introduced, as to exhibit to the public a faithful representation of the National Hall, with its furniture and business during the session of Congress. If the individuals are simply recognized by their acquaintance as likenesses, the whole design of the painting will be answered." [3]

The artist was the son of the Reverend Jedediah Morse, a Congregational minister, and was educated at Andover and Yale. For a few years he studied painting in England under Benjamin West and shared rooms with Washington Allston, whom he considered the coming successor to the aging West, Copley, and Trumbull. On his return to America in 1815 he painted portraits in New England and in Charleston, South Carolina, some of which are fine paintings, as for example his Lafayette in City Hall, New York, and others disappointing, such as his portrait of old John Adams, in the Brooklyn Museum. He became a founder of the

3. Morse, *Key to Morse's Picture*, 4.

National Academy of Design and was its first president for many years, but in later life he devoted more of his time to inventions and to the development of the telegraph and his code.

What of his likenesses in the monumental view of the Old House? In a detail from the large painting (fig. 24) appears a good example, a readily recognizable likeness of Marshall and one without which his iconography would not be complete. He stands with other members of the Supreme Court on a raised platform in the left distance of the picture, in front of a representation of the Declaration of Independence in which can just be distinguished the tiny portraits of Washington, Adams, and Jefferson. Marshall stands between Livingston on his right and Story on his left. The chief justice is unmistakable, though his head is less than two inches in size. The likeness most closely resembles the Harding portrait of 1829 (fig. 44) and the Martin of 1828–1829 (fig. 46).

Morse had high hopes that the picture would be a financial success. But despite public exhibition in Philadelphia, New York, New Haven, and Boston, it failed to attract the public and was finally sold to Sherman Converse, "an English gentleman," for about a thousand dollars. In 1847 it was purchased in London by the artist Daniel Huntington, who was later to be a pallbearer at Morse's funeral in 1872; it then passed to Charles Huntington and in 1911 was acquired for the Corcoran Art Gallery, where it occupies a prominent position as a national historical document.

Chapter 7

Edward F. Peticolas

(b. 1793)

EDWARD F. PETICOLAS (or Petticolas) was the husband of Jane Braddock Peticolas, who painted a portrait of Marshall after one by Cephas Thompson. But Edward himself was a portraitist, and he too painted Marshall, it is believed in 1824. Edward was the most gifted member of a family of artists, and his portrait of the chief justice (fig. 25) is an interesting likeness. If the 1824 date is correct, the portrait stands chronologically between those by Cephas Thompson and Rembrandt Peale, perhaps resembling the former more. It does not appear to be a copy of any known likeness, but is recognizable as Marshall as he must have appeared at the age of sixty-nine.

Like many of the portraits of the chief justice the provenance of the Peticolas likeness is obscure. For years it belonged to the late Malcolm Bruce and hung at Berry Hill Plantation, South Boston, Virginia. Mr. Bruce was a direct descendant of Marshall's and presumably inherited the portrait. At his death on March 30, 1948, an effort was made to acquire the painting for the John Marshall House, but the executors advised that "the portrait will in all probability be sold at Public Auction." [1] The mills of the gods grind slowly. It was not until 1951 that the portrait again came to light when Allen P. Kirby gave it to Lafayette College, Easton, Pennsylvania, with a group of other portraits of "Famous Americans." [2] The list of portraits included in the gift is impressive, but the attribution of some is questionable. Mr. Kirby had acquired the Marshall portrait, and the others, through the aid of E. J. Rousuck, executive vice-president of the Wildenstein Gallery. Among them was a portrait of John Quincy Adams attributed

1. Walter Bruce to Marguerite Stuart Quarles, Secretary of the APVA, Nov. 13, 1948, Association for the Preservation of Virginia Antiquities, Richmond.

2. *Exhibition of Paintings of Famous Americans*, Storm King Art Center Catalog (Mountainville, N.Y., 1961). The portrait was reproduced in *The Kirby Collection of Historical Paintings, Located at Lafayette College, Easton, Pennsylvania* (Easton, Pa., 1963), 24.

25. John Marshall. Oil by Edward F. Peticolas, *ca.* 1824

by Mr. Rousuck to James Frothingham but undoubtedly painted by Charles Bird King. The attribution of the Peticolas Marshall, however, long preceded its passing through the hands of the dealers, and there is no doubt of its authorship. It is a fine portrait showing a new view of Marshall, and it can only be regretted that its origins and early history are not better known.

Chapter 8

The Last Known Likenesses
of "Dearest Polly"

A T SOME INDETERMINATE TIME in her later life, a
small oval portrait of Marshall's wife, Mary—"dearest
Polly," as he continued to call her—was painted by an
artist whose identity was only recently discovered. It is a small
portrait (fig. 26), 4 by 3½ inches by sight in a frame approximately 10 by 9¾ inches. The bonnet and ruffles about the neck
are from the 1820s, a time when Mrs. Marshall would have been
in her late fifties. A great-granddaughter of the chief justice's,
Miss Lizzie Archer of Richmond, gave it to the John Marshall
House, where it hangs today. In 1957 Miss Ellen Harvie Smith
wrote that the frame had never been opened, and thus it had
never been determined whether the painting was by Saint-Mémin,
as many had supposed. In recent years it seemed less likely that
the little portrait was the work of Saint-Mémin, though by whom
it had been painted remained unknown. Finally, in 1972, the
frame was opened, and the portrait was found to be signed
"T. Marshall," presumably John and Polly's son Thomas.

This discovery straightens the record. Another likeness of Mrs.
Marshall (fig. 27) has long been said to have been a copy by
Thomas Marshall of the portrait in figure 26, which, in turn, some
of the family had thought to be by Saint-Mémin. The painting
in figure 27 is much larger, 29½ by 24½ inches, and is no doubt
a copy, with additions, of the small oval; it presents a softer, more
pleasant representation of the subject than the miniature. In both
can be discovered the "Polly" of the 1799 pastel, but both show
her appearing many years older. Time took its toll of "dearest
Polly" as of others, and it is sentimentally reassuring to have the
earlier pastel likeness to remind us how charming the young wife
and mother must have been.

Both of these pictures are now in the John Marshall House, the
latter on loan from Charles E. A. Marshall of New York. Except
for the portrait signed "T. Marshall" (fig. 26) and the one long
believed to have been painted by Thomas Marshall (fig. 27), no
other evidence of his work as a painter has come to light.

26. Mary Willis Marshall. Pen and ink on paper by Thomas
Marshall, *ca.* 1820–1830

27. Mary Willis Marshall. Oil by an unknown artist

Chapter 9

Rembrandt Peale

(1778–1860)

COMPARISONS may be odious, but it would not be difficult to find agreement with the judgment that Rembrandt Peale was the most gifted son of Charles Willson Peale. His two portraits of Jefferson, one painted in 1800 in Philadelphia and now in the White House and the other painted in 1805 in Washington and now in the New-York Historical Society, would alone establish his position as an outstanding portraitist.

Peale's first portrait of Marshall was painted in 1825 (fig. 28). Sometime earlier Marshall had written to him expressing his opinion of Peale's "porthole" portrait of Washington: "I have received your letter of yesterday, and shall, with much pleasure, communicate the impression I received from viewing your Washington. I have never seen a portrait of that great man which exhibited so perfect a resemblance of him. The likeness in features is striking, and the character of the whole face is preserved and exhibited with wonderful accuracy. It is more Washington, himself, than any portrait of him I have ever seen." [1] In the light of such enthusiasm Peale doubtlessly had little trouble in persuading Marshall himself to sit for a portrait, though the exact dates of the sittings are not known. How long Peale kept possession of the resulting portrait is not known either, but by 1858, two years before his death, it was hanging in the Virginia State Library at Richmond. At that time Peale wrote to Captain Montgomery C. Meigs at the Library of Congress suggesting that his portrait of Marshall should be hung as a companion to his porthole likeness of Washington in a suitable place in the then new Senate Chambers.[2] Public bodies are often slow to grasp good opportunities to acquire portraits, and the authorities turned down Peale's suggestion. Time passed, and the portrait was ultimately and fortunately acquired by members of the Association of the Bar of the City of

1. Marshall to Rembrandt Peale, Mar. 10, 1824, quoted in *Niles' Weekly Register,* XXVI (Mar.–Sept. 1824), 37.
2. Peale to Meigs, Dec. 13, 1858, "Library of Congress, 1853–1880, Correspondence Addressed to the Library of Congress," Library of Congress.

28. John Marshall. Oil by Rembrandt Peale, 1825

New York and presented to Chief Justice Salmon P. Chase, at whose death in 1873 it was bequeathed to the Supreme Court.[3]

Justice Joseph Bradley said of this portrait that, "although a fine painting," it "has not been recognized as a good likeness by those who knew the Chief Justice." [4] Another commented that it was "charming as a work of art, but has so little vraisemblance that it might pass for almost anybody as well as the great jurist." [5] We can perhaps draw our own conclusion by comparison with other likenesses of Marshall. Peale's work was sufficiently well

29. John Marshall. Engraving by
unknown artist, 1954

thought of, however, to be used as a model by the Bureau of Engraving and Printing for the forty-cent postage stamp, Series of 1954 (fig. 29), which was taken from a photograph of the portrait (fig. 28) by Harris-Ewing of Washington. The engraving was done by the bureau's engravers, R. M. Bower, C. A. Brooks, and J. S. Edmundson, though it is not clear whether one or all of them worked on it. The result is a fair representation in small of the original.

In 1834, while the porthole portrait was still in Peale's possession, he painted a replica of it (fig. 30). It too is a fine painting,

3. Charles E. Fairman, *Art and Artists of the Capitol of the United States of America* (Washington, D.C., 1927), 361.

4. Joseph P. Bradley, "Saint-Mémin's Portrait of Marshall," *Century Illustrated Monthly Magazine*, XXXVIII (May–Oct. 1889), 778.

5. E. V. Smalley, "The Supreme Court of the United States," *ibid.*, XXV (Nov. 1882–Apr. 1883), 177.

30. John Marshall. Oil by Rembrandt Peale

well executed, even if not showing a familiar likeness of the man. Little is known of the history of this painting. We are told that it was bought from the artist by the Honorable James Humphrey of Brooklyn, New York, at whose death in 1866 it was bequeathed to the Long Island Historical Society.[6] It was reproduced, framed in oval, in the May 1901 issue of the *Green Bag*, a popular magazine for members of the bar. In 1956 it was purchased by the Virginia Museum of Fine Arts, through the Glasgow Fund. It is reproduced here (fig. 30) as it appeared after its 1956 restoration, by which time its oval frame had been removed, thus revealing the whole canvas, 30 by 25 inches.

Harriet Martineau, the sociologist and novelist, wrote a moving "pen-sketch" of a scene in the Supreme Court during Marshall's last years—and perhaps a year after Peale's second painting of him was completed:

At some moments the court presents a singular spectacle. I have watched the assemblage while the Chief-Justice was delivering a judgment, the three justices on either hand gazing at him more like learners than associates; Webster, standing firm as a rock, his large, deep-set eyes wide awake, his lips compressed, and his whole countenance in that intent stillness which instantly fills the eye of a stranger; Clay leaning against the desk in an attitude whose grace contrasts strangely with the slovenly make of his dress, his snuff-box for the moment unopened in his hand, his small gray eye and placid half-smile conveying an expression of pleasure which redeems his face from its usual unaccountable commonness; the Attorney-General (Benjamin F. Butler, of New York), his fingers playing among his papers, his quick, black eye and tremulous lips fixed, his small face, pale with thought, contrasting remarkably with the other two. These men, absorbed in what they are listening to, thinking neither of themselves nor of each other, while they are watched by the group of idlers and listeners around them,—the newspaper corps, the dark Cherokee chiefs, the stragglers from the West, the gay ladies in their waving plumes, and the members of either house that have stepped in to listen,—all these have I seen at one moment constitute one silent assembly, while the mild voice of the aged Chief-Justice sounded through the court.[7]

It is a picture we can see clearly. Marshall, Clay, and Webster are familiar to us through their many portraits. George Catlin and

6. "Accessions of American and Canadian Museums January–March 1956," *Art Quarterly*, XIX (1956), 305, where the portrait is reproduced.
7. Quoted in Smalley, "Supreme Court," *Century Magazine*, XXV (Nov. 1882–Apr. 1883), 176.

C. B. King preserved the likenesses of the Indian chiefs of the day, and even Butler's likeness is not unfamiliar. But it was Marshall as always who dominated the scene, and the artist who produced the two striking likenesses of Jefferson undoubtedly preserved Marshall for us as he saw him.

Chapter 10

John Wesley Jarvis
(1780–1840)

THE JARVIS LIKENESSES of Chief Justice Marshall, represented by nine of the portraits illustrated here (figs. 31–39), raise a familiar question in a study of Marshall's iconography. Which is the original life portrait, and which are replicas by Jarvis or copies by other artists? There are conflicting claims.

The Jarvis portraits fall into two groups. The first comprises six paintings (figs. 31–36), the first five of which share an obvious common source, have comparable backgrounds, and present Marshall at what we can accept as age seventy; yet the sixth (fig. 36) shows the same pose and background but portrays a much younger man.[1] The second group is of two portraits: one (fig. 38) a poor copy of one of the first group and the other (fig. 39) a better copy (or replica) but with a totally different background and an unpleasing likeness. No definite date can be assigned to any of the portraits.

Jarvis was born in England in 1780 and was brought to Philadelphia about 1785. He was early apprenticed to Edward Savage, then moved to New York City, where for some years he was in partnership with Joseph Wood, the miniaturist, an association that perhaps contributed to his irregular and somewhat dissolute life. By 1813 his talent as a portrait painter was well recognized, and late that year he was elected a member of the New-York Historical Society. Within the next four years he painted in full-length six of the distinguished officers who served in the War of 1812, the portraits commissioned for and now hanging in New York's City Hall. The group were Commodores Oliver Hazard Perry, Isaac Hull, and William Bainbridge, Captain Thomas Macdonough, and Generals Jacob Jennings Brown and Joseph Gardner Swift. After 1820 Jarvis lived principally in the South until 1834, when he suffered a disabling stroke that ended his career. He died in New York six years later.

From 1825 to 1827 Jarvis was in Virginia. On October 20, 1825,

1. Fig. 37, the ninth Jarvis likeness, is an engraving of fig. 36.

he wrote to his friend Dr. Samuel Latham Mitchill telling of his social progress in Richmond: "I have had a pleasant and profitable campaign in Virginia. Last week some gentlemen did me the honor to take wine with me and must tell you the names of a few of them, they all know you, some personally—*Governor Pleasants, Chief Justice Marshall,* Mr. Wickham and one of his sons, Coln. Harvey (son in law to Chief), C. Nickolas (Cashier of the U.S. Bank), Coln. Brockenborrow, Wm Roan (grand son of Patrick Henry) and ten or fifteen more. The old Chief staid longer than I have known him to stay out before, for he did not go until Eight in the Eveng and he usually goes away from a frolic at sundown." [2] From this letter it seems clear that Jarvis had been in Marshall's company before, and we can perhaps date his life portrait of the chief justice to this period. The problem is to examine the various Jarvis representations and to attempt to establish their hierarchy.

Harold E. Dickson, author of the definitive volume on Jarvis and his portraits, wrote that after painting the original life portrait, Jarvis made copies for each of Marshall's five sons. Dickson reached his own conclusion as to which of the Marshall portraits was the original, but it appears that he had not seen all the others and did not know of the existence of some of them—at least they are not listed in his register of Jarvis portraits.

Dickson's choice (fig. 31) is the portrait that once belonged to Marshall's youngest son, Edward Carrington Marshall, from whom it descended to his son Jaquelin Ambler Marshall of Markham, Virginia, then to his son Richard Stribling Marshall, of Lexington, Virginia, in 1935, and then to his son Richard Coke Marshall, its present owner. Of this portrait Dickson wrote that it "stands high in his [Jarvis's] output of strong likenesses." [3] The painting was cleaned, subsequent to being photographed as illustrated here, and the neckcloth was partially obliterated. Despite the condition of this illustration, it is an acceptable reproduction for use in comparison with the other portraits. It is a fine, strong likeness of the chief justice, and was reproduced in Nathan Schachner's biography of Aaron Burr. [4] The fact, however, that this portrait belonged to Marshall's youngest son, who was only twenty years old when it is presumed to have been painted,

2. Quoted in Harold E. Dickson, *John Wesley Jarvis: American Painter, 1780–1840, with a Checklist of His Works* (New York, 1949), 288.
3. *Ibid.,* 189.
4. *Aaron Burr: A Biography* (New York, 1937), 405.

31. John Marshall. Oil by John Wesley Jarvis, *ca.* 1825

2. John Marshall. Oil by John Wesley   33. John Marshall. Oil by an unknown
Jarvis   artist

might suggest that it is not the original life portrait but one of the five replicas.

One of the finest of the first group is the portrait now owned by Dr. John Marshall Thayer of Hillsborough, California (fig. 32). He reports that his grandmother, Mrs. William B. Thayer, whose great-grandfather was Marshall's brother Thomas, purchased it in the 1890s, though from whom he knows not. It descended to him from his parents, Mr. and Mrs. William B. Thayer, Jr., of Redlands, California. In 1965 Mrs. Thayer, Jr., corresponded about the portrait with Dickson and sent him a colored photograph about which he wrote: "This is a superb Jarvis portrait, as strong and convincing as any I have seen. Apparently the painter responded to the challenge of his subject." [5] It is not hard to echo this judgment. But this exchange of letters, of course, was many years after the 1949 publication of Dickson's book on Jarvis. If figure 32 is one of the replicas painted for Marshall's sons, presumably Mrs. Thayer purchased it from a Marshall descendant. It discloses the same general treatment of the background (per-

5. John Marshall Thayer to the author, Apr. 29, 1972.

haps improved by artistic license) as figure 31 and maintains an acceptable likeness of the seventy-year-old chief justice. Notice the almond-shaped eyes, the slight droop of the sitter's right eyelid, the way his hair is brushed on his forehead, the several lines in his right cheek and but one in his left, and the highlights on his hair.

Another of the first group, surely stemming from a common source with figures 31 and 32, is the example now owned by the University Club, New York City (fig. 33)—a splendid portrayal of character, and eligible to be either the original or one of the five replicas. Its history, however, is shrouded in obscurity. It does not appear to be signed or inscribed on the front or back, and the University Club says that "its past history does not seem to be readily available." But the Frick Art Reference Library reports that it was purchased for the University Club in 1888 from M. Sullivan Schley (as being by John Trumbull—a poor guess) by subscription of the members of the club. In later years the attribution to Trumbull was understandably questioned by the late Theodore Sizer, the authority on Trumbull,[6] and the portrait is now accepted as by or after Jarvis. It was illustrated, as by Trumbull, in the Century Association's 1937 exhibition catalog, *Portraits Owned by Clubs of New York.*[7] We can only regret that the record of its acquisition in 1888 did not disclose its origins, for it stands on a par with figures 31 and 32 and can share the claim for primacy.

We must now consider the portrait owned by the Valentine Museum in Richmond, Virginia, and on loan to Richmond's 2300 Club (fig. 34). The records of the museum indicate that its artist is unknown but that the portrait was a gift in 1956 of Mrs. Norman Baxter, whose husband's family had owned it for several generations. This record, supplemented by the indication that the canvas is probably contemporary with Jarvis's career, gives this portrait a place in the group of replicas, if not a claim to be the original. The treatment of the background is consistent with the others, the neckcloth is a variation, no two being alike, but the facial expression lacks the firmness and strength of, say, figure 32, and the general impression is of a somewhat younger man.

The Thomas Gilcrease Institute of American History and Art,

6. Frick Art Reference Library to Mrs. William B. Thayer, Jr., July 21, 1964, copy in possession of the author.

7. *Portraits Owned by Clubs of New York, January 9 to February 3, 1937* (New York, 1937), plate 7.

4. John Marshall. Oil by an unknown artist

35. John Marshall. Oil by John Wesley Jarvis

of Tulsa, Oklahoma, owns another example (fig. 35). Here, as is often the case, no information or provenance is available. The institute writes that the picture was acquired by Thomas Gilcrease from Knoedler Galleries in 1958 and that they "have no further information on it"—a not unfamiliar reply from a dealer. Knoedler did not respond to an inquiry about this portrait. The painting itself does not give us much help. The background corresponds to the others, the folds of Marshall's robe on his shoulders compare quite closely with figures 32 and 34, the hair style and highlights are consistent, but the general impression is one of hurried reproduction, perhaps not unexpected if this is one of five replicas. There seems little likelihood it is the original.

The last of this group of six portraits (fig. 36) is now hanging in the East Reception Room of the White House. For many years it belonged to Supreme Court Justice Horace Gray. Professor James B. Thayer of Harvard Law School made an unsuccessful attempt to see Gray's portrait late in 1900 and received an apology from Gray: "I am very sorry that you should have been prevented by the dragon at my door from seeing my portrait of Marshall. But such dragons rarely have, or can be presumed to

36. John Marshall. Oil by John Wesley
Jarvis, 1825

37. John Marshall. Etching and engravin
by Albert Rosenthal, *ca.* 1900

have, any discretion." [8] Gray again wrote to Thayer in 1901, "My
Jarvis portrait, I think, came from a Mr. Morse, of New Orleans. I
bought it from the dealer Barlow here." [9] At the time of the centennial celebration of Marshall's becoming chief justice, Gray
spoke at the memorial celebrations at Richmond. After referring
to a stirring description of Marshall by Horace Binney, Gray said,

Of all the portraits by various artists, that which best accords with
the above description, especially in the "eyes dark to blackness, strong
and penetrating, beaming with intelligence and good nature," is one
by Jarvis (perhaps the best American portrait painter of his time, next
to Stuart), which I have had the good fortune to own for thirty years,
and of which, before I bought it, Mr. Middleton, then the clerk of the
Supreme Court, who had been deputy clerk for eight years under
Chief Justice Marshall, wrote me: "It is an admirable likeness; better
than the one I have, which has always been considered one of the
best." This portrait was taken while his hair was still black, or nearly

8. Gray to J. B. Thayer, Nov. 16, 1900, Thayer Papers, Harvard University Law School, Cambridge, Mass.
9. Gray to J. B. Thayer, May 20, 1901, *ibid.*

so; and, as shown by the judicial robe, and by the curtain behind and above the head, was intended to represent him as sat in court.[10]

The portrait was presented to the White House in 1962, having been acquired from Gray's descendants by Mr. and Mrs. Samuel I. Newhouse. The official guidebook to the White House states that the portrait was "commissioned by Nathan Morse, a friend and prominent New Orleans attorney, was painted in Philadelphia by Jarvis and was completed in the fall of 1825." [11] Justice Gray believed it was commissioned by Morse, without assigning any date to the painting. It is reproduced as the frontispiece to the second volume of Beveridge's *Life of John Marshall,* in which it is stated that "it represents Marshall as he was during his early years as Chief Justice and as he appeared when Representative in Congress and Secretary of State. The Jarvis portrait is by far the best likeness of Marshall during this period of his life." [12]

This statement, of course, raises serious questions. It wasn't until the middle of the first decade of the nineteenth century that Jarvis began to paint portraits seriously, at a time when he lived in New York. No opportunity would seem to have offered itself to Jarvis at that time to paint Marshall; indeed it seems unlikely that Jarvis had ever met Marshall before the painter moved south in the 1820s. It is a puzzle: the portrait certainly shows us a young likeness of Marshall, but at the same time the likeness, except for the apparent age of the sitter, is so close to that of figures 31 to 35 as to make it implausible that this portrait is independent of the others, or that it is the original life portrait. Dickson, who had not seen this version when he wrote his book, correctly commented when he saw a photograph of it, that it "seems to show the subject at a much younger age." [13]

10. From Gray's Memorial Address delivered at Richmond at the request of the Virginia State Bar Association and the Bar Association of the City of Richmond, Feb. 4, 1901, as quoted in John F. Dillon, comp. and ed., *John Marshall: Life, Character and Judicial Services . . .* (Chicago, 1903), I, 90. Daniel Wesley Middleton served as clerk of the Supreme Court from 1863 to 1880 and had been an assistant clerk of the Court from 1825 to 1863. The portrait he owned was fig. 79, a copy of Inman's portrait of Marshall (fig. 73).

11. *The White House, An Historic Guide,* 4th ed. (Washington, D.C., 1913), 56.

12. Albert J. Beveridge, *The Life of John Marshall* (Boston, 1916–1919), II, xv.

13. Dickson to Mrs. W. B. Thayer, May 6, 1965, in possession of Dr. J. M. Thayer, Hillsborough, Calif.

At some time around the turn of the century Albert Rosenthal, the engraver, made a fine reproduction of this portrait in etching and engraving (fig. 37). It appears in four states, with and without Marshall's autograph signature, signed by Rosenthal in the lower right-hand margin, and also containing, within the engraved plate at the lower right-hand corner, Rosenthal's signature in reverse. Like its original, it shows Marshall as a young man, certainly not seventy years of age.

There remain the two portraits comprising the second group. One (fig. 38) is but a poor copy, probably taken from figure 31. Not much is known about it, including the identity of the artist. The John Marshall House Committee of the Association for the Preservation of Virginia Antiquities purchased it from Mrs. J. Addison Price of Germantown, Tennessee, to whom it had been given by a Mrs. Norton. At that time it had a long slit through the face, tradition characteristically claiming that the canvas had been cut by Union soldiers during the Civil War. Whether there be any truth in that tradition, this is at least another of numerous portraits alleged to have been desecrated by Union soldiers. Although the painting has been restored and relined, it is not in good condition. It clearly belongs to the Jarvis type.

Lastly we see a variation of the type (fig. 39) that has a long and distinguished history but that is not an attractive representation of Marshall. It is surely taken from one of the first group, perhaps figure 31, but the artist has made his own changes in background and in certain details of the face and hair. This portrait now belongs to the New York law firm Carter, Ledyard, and Milburn, which received it from Lewis Cass Ledyard III, to whom it had been bequeathed by his father, Lewis Cass Ledyard, Jr. In Mr. Ledyard's will it is described as "the portrait of Chief Justice Marshall which belonged to my great-great-grandfather Brockholst Livingston, who was a Justice of the Supreme Court of the United States at the time that Marshall was Chief Justice thereof." Livingston was on the Court from 1806 to 1823, and his concern for the tribunal on which he sat helped make the Marshall Court a band of brothers. He was the first member of the Marshall Court to die.[14] The back of the painting has a notation disclosing that a restorer sprayed it with a polyvinyl acetate sur-

---

14. Gerald T. Dunne, "Brockholst Livingston," in Leon Friedman and Fred L. Israel, eds., *The Justices of the United States Supreme Court, 1789–1969, Their Lives and Major Opinions* (New York, 1969), I, 394.

. John Marshall. Oil by an unknown artist

39. John Marshall. Oil by John Wesley Jarvis

face coating in May 1954.[15] If owned by Justice Livingston—and there is no reason to doubt the statement in Mr. Ledyard's will—this is an early portrait and may well be a Jarvis replica, though showing greater changes than the others as a group. The face, except for the piercing right eye of the sitter, does not compare favorably with the other examples.

This is all we know of the Jarvis likenesses, fact and rumor, hearsay and tradition; yet the likenesses themselves probably reveal the order of precedence if only we had the perception to read them.

15. Details of the provenance of this portrait are taken from a letter of D. Spencer Byard, a member of the firm of Carter, Ledyard, & Milburn to the author, Dec. 14, 1971.

Chapter 11

Chester Harding
(1792–1866)

ONE of the popular portraitists of the second and third decades of the nineteenth century in Boston and Washington was the self-taught artist Chester Harding, who was born in Conway, New Hampshire, in 1792. In his youth he was a sign painter in Pittsburgh. Later, after trying his hand at portraiture in Paris, Kentucky, Washington, Boston, and Northampton, Massachusetts, he went to England in 1823. There during a three-year residence he established a reputation and attracted a fashionable clientele who accepted him with enthusiasm. On his return to America he worked in Boston, Washington, Richmond, Canada, New Orleans, and Kentucky (where he painted his famous portraits of Daniel Boone). In 1846 he was once more in England and Scotland for a time but came back to America and died in Boston.

Of his talent, an observer or art historian can judge for himself. Upon his death in 1866 some considered him "the most venerable of American artists, and one of the most eminent and accomplished," and "one of the first in point of excellence that America has ever produced; and, in his time, he was the first, without dispute." [1] Elizabeth C. Agassiz, writing to Professor James B. Thayer in 1901 after reading Harding's autobiography, *Egotistigraphy*, commented: "I think he must have had a very attractive personality,—for his artistic gifts could hardly have accounted for his position among the most intelligent and cultivated as well as the most aristocratic people in England." [2]

At the height of his career Harding painted many of the prominent Americans of the day, including Marshall and John Quincy Adams. The earliest notice of his painting the chief justice appears in Adams's diary in March 1828: "Walk to Mr. Harding's lodgings where I gave him a third sitting of about an hour for my

1. The *Boston Evening Transcript*, Apr. 2, 1866, and the *Springfield Republican*, Apr. 1866, quoted in Margaret E. White, ed., *A Sketch of Chester Harding, Artist—Drawn by His Own Hand* (Boston, 1890), 256, 263.
2. Mar. 23, 1901, Thayer Papers, Harvard University Law School, Cambridge, Mass.

portrait. Mr. Greenough was there, waiting for Chief Justice Marshall whose bust he is taking. Mr. Harding is also taking his portrait and those of the other judges of the Supreme Court of the United States and he is painting a picture of the Court itself in Session. The Chief Justice came about nine o'clock, upon which I immediately withdrew." [3] A fortnight later Marshall wrote to his close friend and colleague Justice Joseph Story: "I beg you to accept my portrait for which I sat in Washington to Mr. Harding, to be preserved when I shall sleep with my Fathers as a testimonial of sincere and affectionate friendship. The remaining hundred dollars, you will be so good as to pay to Mr. Harding for the head and shoulders I have bespoke for myself. I shall not wish the portrait designed for myself to be sent to Richmond till I give directions for it to be accompanied by the head Mr. Greenaugh means to cast for me." [4] A month later Marshall again wrote to Story from Richmond that he had received

a letter from Mr. Harding dated the 6th of April informing me that he should leave Washington within a fortnight from that day and requesting me to direct the disposition he should make of the portrait I had requested him to draw for my use. As he had left Washington ten days before his letter reached me I could give no directions on the subject, and have not written to him. I presume he is in Boston. Will you have the goodness to let him know that his letter was not answered because it was not received & that I will thank him if he has left the portrait in Washington to let me know with whom it remains; and, if it is with him to deliver it to you. I shall rely on you to give it house room till the representation of the court in costume is prepared when I must make arrangements to have both, together with the head in plaister, conveyed to this place. [5]

Adams made further reference to the painting of the Court: "Harding has good likenesses of all the justices of the Supreme Court, and he has begun a picture of them, as in session." [6] It would appear from these references that the picture of the Court

3. Diary of John Quincy Adams, Mar. 12, 1828, Adams Papers, Massachusetts Historical Society, Boston.

4. Mar. 26, 1828, Story Papers, Massachusetts Historical Society, Boston. The cryptic mention of "the remaining hundred dollars" probably refers to some missing earlier letter in which Marshall must have sent Story funds from which to pay Harding. For a discussion of Greenough's "head" see chap. 20 below.

5. May 1, 1828, Story Papers.

6. Diary of John Quincy Adams, Apr. 21, 1828, Adams Papers.

in session was to be for Marshall and that it had actually been begun, but it has not been found, nor is it mentioned specifically in Harding's own *Sketch* or *Egotistigraphy*. But Harding wrote of this period: "My visit to Washington, notwithstanding my indisposition, has been one of profit and pleasure. I have had the gratification of seeing a good deal of the great men of the age, particularly Judge Marshall. I am convinced that I shall feel through life that the opportunity to paint the Chief Justice, and at the same time hear his converse, would be ample compensation for my trouble in accomplishing these objects. But over and above all that, I have got portraits of *all* the Supreme Judges." [7] Shortly before Harding left Washington, but after the completion of his portrait of Adams, the president had an opportunity to show his son George not only that portrait but those of the justices of the Supreme Court, remarking that the latter were "good likenesses." [8]

A little more than a year later, in the fall of 1829, Harding, like other artists, went to Richmond at the time of the meeting of the Virginia Constitutional Convention, and there, as he tells us, he painted another portrait of Marshall: "You probably know that I left Boston for Richmond with the intention of *taking off the heads* of the Convention. During my stay in that place, I painted eighteen portraits in all, and amongst them were the two vice-presidents, John Randolph and Chief Justice Marshall again. My visit independent of any pecuniary consideration, was one that I shall long remember with pleasure." [9] Some of Harding's portraits, perhaps including examples painted in Washington earlier in the year, were praised in the Richmond press: "I would invite your readers, who have a taste for the Fine Arts, to visit the painting-rooms of Mr. Harding, just below the Coffee-Room. They will see there the portraits of many of the distinguished men of the nation, Judges of the Supreme Court of the United States —the venerable Carroll—Mr. Pickering—Mr. Webster—Mr. Wirt, etc. The head of the Chief Justice is particularly fine, and true to the original." [10]

7. Harding to S. F. Lyman, May 6, 1828, quoted in White, ed., *Sketch of Chester Harding*, 183.

8. Oliver, *Portraits of John Quincy Adams*, 139.

9. Harding to S. F. Lyman, Feb. 25, 1830, in White, ed., *Sketch of Chester Harding*, 198–199.

10. *Compiler* (Richmond), Oct. 8, 1829, quoted in Valentine Museum, *Richmond Portraits in an Exhibition of Makers of Richmond, 1737–1860* (Richmond, 1949), 221.

It is, then, fairly well established that by the end of 1829 Harding had painted at least three portraits of Marshall, one for Story and one for Marshall (painted in Washington) and the third one painted in Richmond. Story received the one intended for him (fig. 40), and at his death in 1845 it was bequeathed to Harvard. His will, dated January 2, 1843, provided in part: "I give to the President and Fellows of Harvard College, to their use and behoof forever, the following articles, viz: — The portrait of my late excellent friend, Mr. Chief Justice Marshall, by Harding, which was presented to me by the Chief Justice himself." [11] For many years the portrait hung in the dining hall of Memorial Hall at Harvard, and is now in the north lecture room of Langdell Hall of the Harvard Law School.

What of the other two portraits? Three portraits by or attributable to Harding may include the two we seek. One is known to belong to a Marshall descendant in Houston, Texas, but all efforts to obtain a photograph of it have failed. It might well be the one Marshall ordered for himself. Another (fig. 41) now belongs to Washington and Lee University and hangs in the Lee Chapel Museum on the campus in Lexington, Virginia. It was bequeathed to the university by Dr. William Newton Mercer of New Orleans, who died in 1874 and whose will described the portrait as being an "original by Harding." [12] A collector of American portraits and perhaps a friend or admirer of Harding's, Dr. Mercer bequeathed to the Redwood Library and Athenaeum of Newport, Rhode Island, of which he was for many years a trustee, portraits of John Quincy Adams and Daniel Webster, both by Harding. [13] Just when this Marshall portrait was painted is not known, but it could well be the one completed in Richmond in 1829; Harding might have sold it to Mercer with the Adams and Webster portraits when he visited New Orleans. As a likeness it stands up very well beside Harding's monumental portrait of Marshall belonging to the Boston Athenaeum (fig. 44). A copy or replica of it done in pastel, an oval 26 by 20¾ inches, was formerly in the collection of William Grant of New Orleans and was inherited by his daughter, Mrs. Alexander Leslie Black of New Orleans, prior to 1933. Its

11. William W. Story, ed., *Life and Letters of Joseph Story* . . . (Boston, 1851), II, 553.
12. Will on file, docket no. CDC 66162, Civil District Court for the Parish of Orleans, New Orleans. Extracts are among the Thayer Papers.
13. George Champlin Mason, *Annals of the Redwood Library and Athenaeum, Newport, R.I.* (Newport, R.I., 1891), 337.

40. John Marshall. Oil by Chester Harding, 1828

41. John Marshall. Oil by Chester Harding, *ca.* 1829

whereabouts are not known, but the Frick Art Reference Library has a photograph of it. The original (fig. 41) was reproduced as the frontispiece to the May 1901 issue of the *Green Bag*.

Horace Gray of Boston, who had become an associate justice of the Supreme Court in 1881, learned of the Washington and Lee portrait from Professor Thayer and saw it or a photograph of it. He wrote Thayer that the portrait was new to him and very interesting and that it "like all the other good portraits upsets Story's early Democratic description of 'eyes small and twinkling.'"[14] Gray strongly admired Marshall and long owned a very striking portrait of him by Jarvis (fig. 36), mentioned above.

A third portrait that might qualify as one of the two we seek is now possessed by Tulane University at New Orleans. It came to the university by gift in June 1889 of Mrs. Eustace Surget of

14. Story, ed., *Life and Letters of Joseph Story*, I, 166.

42. John Marshall. Oil attributed to Chester Harding,
ca. 1829

Bordeaux, France, as an addition to the so-called Linton-Surget
Art Collection, which had been presented in May of that year
to the city of New Orleans and was placed on permanent loan to
Tulane.[15] This portrait (fig. 42) has always been attributed to
Harding and bears a close resemblance to his other likenesses of
Marshall. Nothing is known of its provenance, but there is a certain curious coincidence in the New Orleans connection. It is
Marshall at the same time in life as figures 40 and 41. It could
perhaps be the Richmond portrait of 1829 or even a likeness
painted for the purpose of including the head in the great pro-
jected painting of the Supreme Court "as in session." There is no

15. Tulane University Library to the author, Nov. 4, 1971.

43. John Marshall. Oil by John Cranch

difficulty in accepting it as by Harding, whether as an original or modified replica.

The Tulane portrait is probably the source of John Cranch's portrait of Marshall (fig. 43), which now belongs to Washington University, St. Louis, Missouri, as a gift from the late Henry Ware Eliot. Eliot had also owned Cranch's copy of Gilbert Stuart's last portrait of John Adams, and it too was given to Washington University by Eliot's widow.[16] Cranch surely copied the Harding portrait at Tulane for the configuration of Marshall's robe; the head is, with artistic license, perhaps drawn from both the Tulane

16. Oliver, *Portraits of John Quincy Adams*, 195.

portrait (fig. 42) and the Boston Athenaeum portrait (fig. 44). Cranch's portrait was recently reproduced in a reprint edition of Dunlap's *History of the Arts of Design in the United States.*[17]

The next occasion for Harding to paint Marshall arose following the action taken by the trustees of the Boston Athenaeum in accordance with a resolution adopted December 8, 1829: "Voted, that the sum of two hundred dollars be appropriated for a portrait of Chief Justice Marshall by Mr. Harding, and that the Vice-President of this institution be a committee to request Judge Marshall to sit for the same."[18] That the matter was not one to be treated lightly will appear from the following exchange of letters. On January 3, 1830, Francis C. Gray, vice-president of the Athenaeum, wrote to Harding at Washington:

> The Trustees of the Boston Athenaeum having voted to request Chief Justice Marshall to permit his portrait to be taken by you for that Institution, I wrote to him on the subject and have received his answer, complying with the request, this morning—I thought it most respectful to obtain this consent before applying to you. I have now to request that you will undertake this Commission and wait upon the Chief Justice for that purpose. You will, of course, consult his convenience entirely with regard to the time and place of sitting. We doubt not that you will give us a painting which shall be a faithful representation of the original and not unworthy of yourself.
>
> The Trustees have appropriated 200 dollars for this purpose. If you are not satisfied with this sum (though we presume you will be) you will please to write me on the subject. But do not on that account delay proceeding with the work.
>
> Very truly Dr. Sir your friend and Servt
>
> F. C. Gray
>
> P.S. You recollect our Portrait of West, a three quarter length, the canvas of which is 4 feet 10 inches high and 4 feet wide within the frame. Would it not be well to make yours a pendant of this? Unless you think some other size would be really better. We expect a first rate picture and hope you will not stint the size nor neglect the execution on any account.[19]

Despite the condescending tone of Gray's letter, Harding responded promptly and bravely:

17. William Dunlap, *History of the Rise and Progress of the Arts of Design in the United States* (New York, 1969 [orig. publ. Boston, 1834]), II, opposite 447.

18. Records of the Boston Athenaeum, Boston.

19. Letterbook, 1822–1838, Boston Athenaeum.

Your letter communicating the resolution of the Trustees of the Athenaeum respecting the portrait of Chief Justice Marshall has been received, and I assure you I feel most sensibly the honor they do me in selecting me as the artist; and that I shall spare no pains to do justice to so noble a subject.

I feel more solicited in regard to the size, than the price of this picture. *$250* is my price for a "Bishop half-length" (the size you recommend) and $500 for a full-length. You say the sum voted for the purpose is fixed at *$200*. I have long wished to paint a whole-length of some distinguished man, and a more favorable opportunity to gratify that wish is not likely to occur. I am therefore willing to paint the picture at full length for the sum voted if, when the picture is presented the committee does not think it worth more—or if they cannot consistently with their duty as trustees give more.

I shall therefore avail myself of the latitude given me in your instructions, and procede with the picture with as much dispatch as the leisure of the Chief Justice will allow, hoping, that while it gratifies my ambitions it will be satisfactory to the gentlemen of the Athenaeum.[20]

Harding went straight to work, and we have this account of one sitting by Marshall:

When I was ready to draw the figure into his picture, I asked him, in order to save time, to come to my room in the evening. . . . An evening was appointed; but he could not come until after the "consultation," which lasts until about eight o'clock. . . . It was a warm evening and I was standing on my steps waiting for him, when he soon made his appearance, but, to my surprise, without a hat. I showed him into my studio, and stepped back to fasten the front door, when I encountered [several gentlemen] who knew the judge very well. They had seen him passing by their hotel in his hatless condition, and with long strides, as if in great haste, and had followed, curious to know the cause of such a strange appearance. . . . He said that the consultation lasted longer than he expected, and he hurried off as quickly as possible to keep his appointment with me.

On leaving, the account continues, Harding offered him a hat, but he declined it: "Oh no, it is a warm night; I shall not need one." [21]

Matters progressed rapidly; on March 9, Isaac P. Davis, a trustee of the Athenaeum, was authorized to procure a frame for the "portrait of Judge Marshall now painting by Harding"; in

20. Jan. 15, 1830, Boston Athenaeum; quoted in Mabel Munson Swan, *The Athenaeum Gallery, 1827–1873* (Boston, 1940), 119–120.

21. James B. Thayer, "John Marshall," *Atlantic Monthly,* LXXXVII (1901), 339–340.

August the bill of John Doggett and Company, Boston's leading "Picture Framer," was paid in the amount of $81.50; on July 12, Harding was paid the sum of $350 (a New England compromise), and the great picture (fig. 44) came into the Athenaeum's possession. It is a striking likeness and a magnificent portrait, monumental in size, 94 by 58 inches, and now hangs in the Athenaeum, in the vestibule—which, as historian Mabel M. Swan noted hyperbolically, looks almost as if it had been built about the portrait. This is the chief justice, aged seventy-five, as he appeared only a few weeks following the last meeting of the giants, at which he and Madison had escorted the aged ex-president Monroe to the chair, and at which Marshall himself had been so effective in reconciling differences and effecting reasonable compromises.

Harding, who admired Marshall tremendously, was understandably pleased with the outcome and all the events leading up to it, as appears from his own recollections:

I consider it a good picture. I had great pleasure in painting *the whole* of such a man. . . . I again met Judge Marshall in Richmond whither I went during the sittings of the convention for amending the Constitution. He was a leading member of a quoit club, which I was invited to attend. The battle ground was about a mile from the city, in a beautiful grove. I went early, with a friend, just as the party were beginning to arrive. I watched for the coming of the old chief. He soon approached with his coat on his arm, and hat in his hand, which he was using as a fan. He walked directly up to a large bowl of mint julep, which had been prepared, and drank off a tumbler full of the liquid, smacked his lips, and then turned to the company with a cheerful "How are you, gentlemen?" He was looked upon as the best pitcher of the party, and could throw heavier quoits than any other member of the club. The game began with great animation, there were several ties; and before long I saw the great chief justice of the Supreme Court of the United States, down on his knees, measuring the contested distance with a straw, with as much earnestness as if it had been a point of law; and if he proved to be in the right, the woods would ring with his triumphant shout. What would the dignitaries of the highest court of England have thought, if they had been present.[22]

At the time Professor James B. Thayer was preparing his centenary account of Marshall, Edward E. Hall of Matunuck, Rhode Island, wrote to him: "The Antiquarian Society has printed the diary of Christopher Baldwin. Have you seen it? He says after an interview with Chester Harding that Harding believed in

22. Chester Harding, *My Egotistigraphy* (Cambridge, Mass., 1866), 144.

44. John Marshall. Oil by Chester Harding, 1829

Phrenology (then new). Harding told Baldwin that he always measured the heads of his sitters—that Marshall's head was the largest he had ever measured and Webster's the next." [23] Harding's daughter Margaret E. White had less to say: "I am sorry to say I can give you no information about Judge Marshall's pictures. To my knowledge my father never signed a picture, nor did I ever know him to make any note of his works nor even to keep any account of money received in payment for his portraits. . . . I am constantly applied to for information about one or another portrait, but, alas! my answer always has to be the same." [24] On the other hand, Edward W. Emerson, who had heard Thayer deliver his centenary address, wrote: "I am glad to know of our National Wealth in having had such a man of whom until that day I knew little beyond his beautiful face and prescence as rendered by Harding and that he was a man of weight and eminence in his times." [25]

Marshall himself was flattered by the Athenaeum's desire to have his portrait painted. In April 1809 he had been nominated as a corresponding member of the Massachusetts Historical Society by Joseph McKean, the society's cabinet keeper, and was duly elected in August. [26] A quarter of a century later he wrote to Story:

> In looking over some old papers the other day to determine how many of them were worthy of being committed to the flames, I found a totally forgotten letter (you need not communicate this) from the Historical Society of Massachusetts (or Boston), announcing that I had been elected an honorary member. To show my gratitude for this distinction, I ask them to accept my book,—a poor return indeed, but the only one I can make.
>
> You know what a compliment has been paid me by your Athenaeum. I have been truly flattered by it, and hope the society will receive my book,—not surely as anything like an equivalent, but as a testimonial of my grateful sense of the favorable sentiment that society has manifested for me. The widow's mite, you know, proved the heart more than the rich gifts of the wealthy. [27]

23. Aug. 22, 1901, Thayer Papers.
24. Margaret E. White to James B. Thayer, Nov. 29, 1900, *ibid.*
25. Edward H. Emerson to J. B. Thayer, Feb. 10, 1901, *ibid.*
26. Entries for Apr. 27, Aug. 29, 1809, Records of the Society, Pt. III (1804–1825), Mass. Hist. Soc.
27. Reproduced in Massachusetts Historical Society, *Proceedings,* 2d Ser., XIV (1900–1901), 355–356.

There is a pleasant confusion of institutions in this letter, but Marshall's appreciation is manifest. The *Proceedings* of the Historical Society reveal that at a special meeting held on June 5, 1833, the librarian, Joseph Willard, "presented the second edition of Marshall's *Washington* with [a] letter from the author."[28]

The portrait was cleaned and varnished in 1905, remounted and cleaned again in 1909 at a cost of $125, and exhibited in 1950 in a National Gallery of Art exhibition, "Makers of History in Washington," commemorating the sesquicentennial of the city of Washington.

No sooner had Harding delivered the portrait to the Athenaeum than we find him trying to borrow it. He wrote to Dr. George Hayward: "I am desirous of having the portrait of Chief Justice Marshall at my room for a short time that I may be enabled to finish the copy which I commenced of it at Washington, before I sent the Picture to the Athenaeum. Also that I may do a little to the original which I have discovered will improve it. Can you assist me in obtaining the picture. If you can you will oblige me much."[29] His request was granted the following day. Seventeen years later the copy (or more properly the replica) came to light in an appropriate manner. A group of prominent Bostonians and professors at the Harvard Law School raised a sum sufficient to purchase the replica from Harding and give it to Harvard, where it now hangs in the great reading room at Langdell Hall opposite a portrait of similar size of Justice Oliver Wendell Holmes. Today we know how it was purchased and by whom, but when Professor Thayer was at work in 1900, it was not at all clear. Only after considerable research did Thayer discover the origin of the replica, from a letter from Allen Danforth, comptroller of Harvard College:

Upon receipt of your letter of Nov. 29 I concluded to examine the Donation Book itself, without using the indexes, which I knew made no reference to the portrait. I find the following entry under date of March 27, 1847: — "Donation of Chief Justice Marshall's Portrait — the following is a copy of the subscription paper drawn up and circulated by Prof. Greenleaf.

'It is proposed to purchase the full length portrait of the late Chief Justice Marshall by Harding and to place the same in the Law School

28. *Ibid.*, 1st Ser., I (1791–1835), 471.
29. Aug. 7, 1830, Correspondence, Boston Athenaeum.

of Harvard College; and for this purpose the undersigned engaged to
pay the sums set opposite to their respective names.

S. Greenleaf	$10	Edward Blake	$ 5
W. Kent	10	F. Loring	5
Theron Metcalf	5	W. Gray	5
C. G. Loring	10	W. Dehon	5
J. Mason	10	F. C. Watts	5
B. R. Curtis	10	B. W. Nichols	2
Joseph Ball	10	John Lowell	5
Richard Fletcher	10	W. G. Russell	2
R. Choat	5	Henry G. Parker	3
			117

In the records of the Corporation's meeting of March 27, 1847 is the
following vote: — "Voted: — That the thanks of the Corporation be presented to the gentlemen who have subscribed for the purchase of a
full length portrait of the late Chief Justice Marshall."

Aware of the problems he had encountered in his research, Mr.
Danforth went on to say: "In the index to the Donation Book
each subscriber's name, and the amount of his subscription towards this portrait, are duly entered, but without knowing who
the subscribers toward the portrait were, one could get no clue to
the gift. We evidently need a subject index in addition to the
index of givers names, and this index and a full index to the
Corporation's records will, I hope, be started soon." [30]

Today there is no longer any doubt as to the origin of the portrait. Due to Professor Thayer's interest, there now hangs beneath
the portrait, neatly framed, the original list of subscribers with
their signatures. The subscription is dated "September 2d 1846,"
and the cost is stated as

Price	$ 100
Expence	15
	$ 115

Before or after each name (and in a few instances both before
and after) is added the word "paid" or "pd," except for F. Loring.
Assuming that Mr. Loring paid, there would have been an over-
subscription of two dollars. The replica is a splendid duplication
of the original, $95^{5}/_{16}$ by $59^{1}/_{4}$ inches, and is an outstanding ornament to Langdell Hall.

30. Danforth to J. B. Thayer, Nov. 30, 1900, Thayer Papers.

That this likeness had a popular appeal is borne out by the December 1891 issue of the *Green Bag*. It reproduced the Athenaeum example as a frontispiece, and on the opposite page was tipped in a flyer advertising that "an enlarged copy of the portrait of Chief Justice Marshall which forms the frontispiece of this number will be *presented to every subscriber remitting the amount of his subscription for 1892 on or before January 1, 1892. . . .* It will make an attractive addition to every lawyer's portrait gallery." The likeness was again used in the February 1901 issue of the *Green Bag*.[31]

Many years later, in 1924, artist Benjamin F. Landis made a copy of the Athenaeum portrait, 84 by 56 inches in size, which Elisha P. Cronkhite presented to the Merchants Club, New York City. It now hangs in the club's rooms at 26 Thomas Street. Mr. Cronkhite, who attended the club's fiftieth anniversary luncheon in 1901, was one of the principal partners of Smith, Hogg, and Company, an old-line commission house that largely sold gray goods from New England mills. The Merchants Club has no records relating to the gift of the portrait; but it is a well-executed copy of Harding's original.

Professor Thayer's interest in Marshall proved contagious in 1900. Bruton Parish Church in Williamsburg in a burst of enthusiasm took under consideration the installation of a Marshall memorial window. The Reverend W. T. Roberts, rector of the church and president of the "Order of Jamestown 1607," wrote to Thayer: "I am also more than grateful to learn of your success in securing subscriptions to the Marshall Memorial window. I feel assured of the success of this enterprise."[32] Thayer himself had agreed to subscribe $25 and had apparently received comparable pledges from "Mr. Leveret, Mr. Olney, Mr. Fisk and M. F. Dickinson Jr." But progress was slow. The next year Roberts wrote again: "While in Williamsburg last Spring, you kindly offered to aid me in bringing the matter of a window in memory of Chief Justice Marshall to be placed in Bruton Church, before the American Bar Association. . . . I have secured the indorsement of leading members of the Va. Bar Association including the names of Hon. L. L. Lewis, Pres. of the Association, Attorney-General Montague and former Gov. Charles F. O'Farrell. . . . I enclose

---

31. *The Green Bag: An Entertaining Magazine for Lawyers*, XIII (1901), 57.
32. Feb. 21, 1901, Thayer Papers.

a copy of the paper as signed by the gentlemen above named and others." The enclosure, dated at Old Point Comfort, July 9, 1900, follows:

We, the undersigned members of the Va. Bar Association, do hereby cordially endorse the proposition to place in Bruton Church, Williamsburg, a stained glass window in memory of John Marshall of Va., the great Chief Justice of the United States of America. We believe that such a window will be a fitting testimonial of our reverence for John Marshall, the Christian believer, that it will be a perpetual inspiration to the youth of Va. who annually gather in the halls of the venerable College of William & Mary—the Alma Mater of John Marshall; and that it will bear witness to a truth that the religion of Christ has always commanded the homage of the world's most regal intellects.
Wm. A. Anderson, Pres., Va. Bar Association
L. L. Lewis, Pres. Elect, "   "   "
former Pres. Va. Court of Appeals
Jno. A. Coke, Richmond, Va.
John Goode, Former Solicitor General, U.S.
Geo. L. Christian, Judge Corporation Court, Richmond, Va.
J. M. Miller, Judge Corporation Court, Petersburg, Va.
Allen R. Honchel, Judge Corporation Court, Norfolk, Va.
A. J. Montague, Attorney-General of Virginia
Chas. T. O'Ferroll, Former Gov. of Virginia [33]

In 1904 an engraving was made of Marshall—head and shoulders—by Albert Rosenthal (fig. 45) inscribed: "Engraved by Albert Rosenthal, Phila. 1904 from the painting by Chester Harding in the Athenaeum, Boston, Mass. Published for the subscribers to the John Marshall Memorial Window to be placed in Bruton Church, Williamsburg, in commemoration of the centennial year of John Marshall's appointment as Chief Justice of the United States." And then, by good fortune, an art historian intervened. The minutes of the Vestry of Bruton Parish Church for April 8, 1905, contain a letter from the Reverend William B. Huntington, rector of Grace Church in New York City, to the Reverend William A. R. Goodwin, a member of Bruton's advisory committee, saying, in part: "If stained glass is to be employed at all in the restoration of a colonial church, I should say it ought, by all means, to be of English make. I should gravely deprecate the admission of any window of the so-called Tiffany type. . . . Let me add, however, that I am fully in agreement with you in

33. Roberts to J. B. Thayer, Aug. 22, 1902, *ibid.*

45. John Marshall. Etching by Albert Rosenthal, 1904

deprecating any stained glass whatsoever." [34] That did it; there the matter stands today, in Bruton Parish Church.

But memorial stained-glass windows still have a popular appeal. The Washington Cathedral is planning a "Christian Statement window" that will include John Marshall, the glass to be designed by the English artist Patrick Reyntiens. Upon inquiry as to which portrait likeness of Marshall was to be followed, the reply was that Mr. Reyntiens works in a style of stained-glass making which is "both stunning and very strikingly contemporary," that his work does not call for the "attention paid to correctness of historical detail which is found in most traditional academic stained glass," and that he will probably use "an impressionistic style in portraying the Marshall figure." [35] Alas!

34. Mar. 20, 1905, in Apr. 8, 1905, Vestry Minutes, Bruton Parish Church, Williamsburg, Va.

35. Gary Thomas Scott, research assistant to the clerk of the works, Washington Cathedral, to the author, Feb. 8, 1972.

Chapter 12

John Blennerhassett Martin

(1797–1857)

TWO INTERESTS ruled the life of John Blennerhassett Martin: his art and his church. As an engraver, lithographer, and artist he made a reputation that will survive, and through his work he was able in his lifetime to support a large family in minimum comfort. At the same time, the Presbyterian church played an important part in his life. As a devoted and active church member, he must have been gratified by the stroke of fortune that made four of his sons Presbyterian ministers. A fifth died as he was answering the same call. It is not surprising, therefore, that many of Martin's engravings embellished books on religion, such as John D. Blair's *Sermons*, Edward Bickersteth's *A Scripture Help*, and others.[1] But he was also an able portraitist.

Born in Ireland, Martin emigrated to America in 1815 when only eighteen years old; two years later he was firmly settled in Richmond. Like so many other artists, he painted several portraits of Marshall—four, we are told—and more than seven of the Martin type are known. To identify the original and to determine just when it was painted becomes our problem. We may fairly start with the Martin likeness that has the earliest acceptable provenance.

In 1902 the University of Virginia was the fortunate recipient of a portrait of the chief justice by Martin (fig. 46) that gives us a good starting point in unraveling the tangle of Martin portraits. The occasion was celebrated with appropriate pomp and ceremony, and its memory preserved in a pamphlet entitled *Presentation of a Portrait of Chief-Justice Marshall to the University of Virginia, June 18, 1902*. The presentation was made in behalf of the donor, John Langborne Williams, M.A., by Judge Lunsford L. Lewis, former president of the Virginia Court of Appeals, and was accepted on behalf of the university by William Minor Lile, professor of law. The pamphlet reveals that Thomas A. Rust of Rich-

---

1. *Sermons Collected from the Manuscripts of the Late Rev. John D. Blair* (Richmond, 1825); Edward Bickersteth, *A Scripture Help, Designed to Assist in Reading the Bible Profitably* (New York, 1828).

46. John Marshall. Oil by John Blennerhassett Martin, *ca.* 1828

mond was, as a young man, a great admirer of Marshall's and in 1828 or 1829 persuaded him to sit to the Richmond artist Martin. Rust kept the resulting portrait in his possession until 1859 when, upon giving up housekeeping, he sold it to John W. Davies. In 1901 John Langborne Williams purchased the portrait from Davies's son through J. J. English of the Bell Book Company. At that time Mr. Williams received a letter (reproduced in the pamphlet) from Rust's son in which he told of his father commissioning the Marshall portrait and also of Martin painting, at the same time, a portrait of Thomas Rust, which was still in the son's possession. The pamphlet also quotes from a letter of the donor: "Miss Anne Harvie, granddaughter of Judge Marshall, tells me that when she was a child Mrs. Francis Gwathmey, who had known the old Judge familiarly, took her down to Mr. John B. Martin's studio to show her a portrait of her grand-father, which she said was excellent." It is quite likely that figure 46 represents the portrait commended by Mrs. Gwathmey. Here we have tradition, memory, a few letters, and a fine portrait; a plausible story in view of the fact that there is no strong conflicting evidence.

Proceeding chronologically, the next portrait attributed to Martin is said to have been painted in 1834 and is probably not a life portrait. The Frick Art Reference Library has a photograph of a portrait that belonged many years ago to a Mrs. S. P. Lees of High Bridge, New York, stated to have been signed by "J. B. Martin 1834." It is a larger painting, 50 by 40 inches, showing a full-length figure seated at a table on which are books and pen and ink. The portrait itself has not been located, but from the photograph it appears to be a replica of the 1828 head (fig. 46) with the full figure and background added. This portrait was probably the source of Alonzo Chappel's engraving (fig. 52) below.

Next in date is a lost portrait of which a photograph also has been preserved. The photograph, reproduced here as figure 47, was made by the photographers J. H. Schaefer and Son of Baltimore and was given to the Frick Art Reference Library in 1938 by Joseph E. Byrnes, clerk of the Supreme Bench of Baltimore City. At that time the late J. Hall Pleasants, the distinguished art historian, informed the Frick Art Reference Library that the portrait had been purchased from Thomas C. Ruckle before March 30, 1840, by the Bar Library Company of Baltimore and that in 1935 it was still hanging in the courthouse in Baltimore. He added, "Whether this is a copy of some well known portrait by

47. John Marshall. Oil by James L. Wattles, prior to 1840

the Baltimore artist, Thomas C. Ruckle, or is a painting by someone else which he picked up and sold to the Bar Association, I do
not know." [2] In 1971 Michael Renshaw, librarian of the Bar Library of Baltimore, informed me that its records indicated that
the portrait had been painted by James L. Wattles, a local artist.
Mr. Renshaw also wrote: "The Marshall portrait seems to have
been destroyed during a renovation of the Court House in the
'50's. A damn shame!"—a sentiment we can echo.[3] The situation is
somewhat confused by these two attributions, but Renshaw's
records seem to establish Wattles as its author. But whence the
likeness of Marshall? For answer to this question we turn elsewhere.

Three other likenesses of Marshall attributable to, or after,
Martin are available for consideration. By Act of Congress passed
August 30, 1890, "one thousand dollars, or so much thereof as
may be necessary" was appropriated "to enable the marshall of
the Supreme Court of the United States under the direction of the
court, to obtain the oil portrait of Chief-Justice Marshall, to be
hung in the robing room with those of the other deceased Chief
Justices already there." [4] The matter was brought to the attention
of (or perhaps initiated by) Justice Joseph P. Bradley, "who was
able to procure it [the portrait] from a relative of Chief Justice
Marshall, such relation furnishing the information that it was considered by the family to be the best known portrait of Mr. Marshall." This becomes a familiar claim and may be entitled to no
more notice than the information from the same source that the
portrait was "painted by Martin in 1814." [5] The portrait (fig. 48)
is a provocative likeness of Marshall—one not seen before. Leaving it in limbo for a few moments, let us look at another.

William L. Marbury of Baltimore, whose great-great-grandfather was Charles Marshall, brother of the chief justice, inherited
a portrait of Marshall (fig. 49) that had been given to his father
in 1910 by Marbury's mother. She had purchased it at an auction
in Baltimore from the estate of a Baltimore lawyer, whose name
is forgotten but who was not believed to be connected with the
chief justice. The purchase was made by Mrs. Marbury for her

2. Quoted in a letter from the Frick Art Reference Library to the author,
Dec. 15, 1971.
3. Renshaw to the author, Dec. 1, 1971.
4. U.S., *Statutes at Large*, XXVI, 410.
5. Charles E. Fairman, *Art and Artists in the Capitol of the United
States of America* (Washington, D.C., 1927), 364.

48. John Marshall. Oil by John Blennerhassett Martin, *ca.* 1834

husband because of his descent from the chief justice's brother Charles. Nothing more has been discovered of the origin of the Marbury portrait.[6]

A third likeness (fig. 50) has even less of a provenance. Owned by Washington University in St. Louis, Missouri, this portrait is clearly of the second Martin type. Nothing is known of its history or how it came to the university. It is oil on canvas, 30¼ by 25 inches. It can be compared with figure 49 and reveals at least a common source; the same chair is visible behind Marshall's left shoulder and the column at his right is similar to that in figure 49 but has been moved farther out of the picture. It exhibits a cer-

6. William L. Marbury to the author, Oct. 4, 1971.

49. John Marshall. Oil attributed to John Blennerhassett Martin,
ca. 1834

tain crudeness suggesting that it is a copy and not an original,
but this may be due to the poor condition of the portrait at the
time it was photographed.

The lost Baltimore example (fig. 47) can, I believe, be accepted
as a modified copy of the Marbury portrait (fig. 49). Compare,
for example, the ends of the tie, the shape of the lapel of the coat
on each side of the tie, the small fold in the coat below the right
shoulder, the sideburns on the sitter's right cheek protruding in
the same manner. There are too many similarities for a coincidence. If we are correct in believing that James Wattles copied
the Marbury portrait, it would seem to strengthen figure 49's
standing as a Martin original or replica.

50. John Marshall. Oil by an unknown artist

Two other likenesses remain to be considered. Records show that Douglas H. Thomas of Baltimore, who owned other portraits of Marshall, at one time owned a portrait of the Martin type (fig. 51). From Thomas it passed to his daughter, Mrs. Robert H. Stevenson, Jr., of Boston; then to Buchanan Schley of New York, late of Mrs. John Ridgely's Baltimore home, Hampton; then to Cornelius Michaelson, a New York dealer. It was sold at Rains Gallery on May 8, 1935, lot 79, for $300, and restored and sold at Parke Bernet, April 6, 1960, lot 82, for $2,700. But it has dropped from sight.

Last, as a sort of confirmatory bit of evidence, we must see the engraving by Alonzo Chappel in 1863 (fig. 52), also reproduced

John Marshall. Oil attributed to John Blennerhassett Martin

52. John Marshall. Engraving by Alonzo Chappel, *ca.* 1863

in the *Century.*[7] Chappel always used a free hand in his portraits, and we have to take some of his embellishments with a grain of salt. His likeness, however, though at first blush resembling Wattles's copy (fig. 47), probably stems from Mrs. Lees's portrait. The head is closer to figure 46, from which Mrs. Lees's portrait was taken, than the later heads. The column is a feature common to almost all of this group; the capitol at Richmond is added for sentimental or historical reasons, and carelessly added in that the overhang of the eaves is made to appear on the near side of the column, an unconscious *trompe l'oeil.*

This, then, is all that has so far come to light. An educated guess would place the known Martin examples in this order:

1. Figure 46, at the University of Virginia, 1828–1829
2. Mrs. Lees's large portrait, about 1834

7. E. V. Smalley, "The Supreme Court of the United States," *Century Illustrated Monthly Magazine,* XXV (Nov. 1882–Apr. 1883), opposite p. 163.

3. Figure 49, the Marbury portrait, about 1834

4. Figure 48, the Supreme Court portrait, about 1834 (though mistakenly said to be 1814)

5. Figure 51, the Douglas H. Thomas portrait, about 1834

6. Figure 47, the Wattles copy of figure 49, before 1840

7. Figure 50, the Washington University example, date unknown but probably an early copy or replica

8. Figure 52, Chappel's engraving of 1863

Chapter 13

Beverley Waugh
Robert Ball Hughes
(1806–1868)

I N RICHMOND, VIRGINIA, on August 6, 1881, the *Standard* carried a column headed "Notes and Queries," which contained the following announcement:

A WAX PORTRAIT IN BASSO-RELIEVO OF CHIEF-JUSTICE MARSHALL

There has just been presented to the Virginia Historical Society by the Rev. Horace Edwin Hayden, Wilkesbarre, Pennsylvania, an interesting memorial of Chief-Justice John Marshall—a wax figure of him in basso-relievo which Mr. Hayden states "was executed by the artist Beverley Waugh some forty or more years ago. My father, Edwin P. Hayden, Esq., a lawyer of Howard County, Maryland, was a great admirer of the Chief-Justice. When I was a boy I remember that this figure, handsomely framed, hung in my father's office. Before he died, which was in 1850, he presented me with the figure, which was then 'full length,' giving the Chief-Justice's style of dress as I have read it described in print. In my frequent removals since then the lower part of the figure has been broken into so many fragments that I was obliged to cut it off at the waist. It represented the Chief-Justice in the attitude of one delivering a speech, and I judge the likeness is very accurate." The execution of the figure exhibits delicacy of treatment and artistic excellence, and is unmistakeably a delineation from life. The present length of the figure is four inches and the color of the material white. The hair is arranged in a cue, the style of the last century, in which style it was worn, with the accompanying dress of the flapped waistcoat and knee breeches, by the Chief-Justice during life.

This is an excellent description of the small wax likeness (fig. 53), and a difficult one to augment. The figure is believed to have been made in the 1830s. The gift is recorded in the minutes of the Virginia Historical Society dated January 4, 1882, and the piece is listed in Weddell's *Portraiture in the Virginia Historical Society.*[1]

The peregrination required by the profession of the Reverend Mr. Hayden (1837–1917) occasioned the destruction of the lower part of the figure, which presumably contained the artist's signature. We can get some idea of what it looked like from a

1. Alexander Wilbourne Weddell, *Portraiture in the Virginia Historical Society* (Richmond, 1945), 130.

53. John Marshall. Wax bas-relief by Beverley Waugh, *ca.* 1830

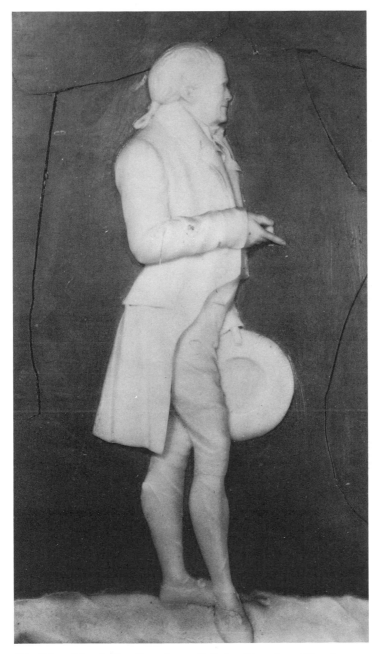

54. John Marshall. Wax bas-relief by Beverley Waugh, *ca.*
1830

practically identical counterpart (fig. 54), now owned by Miss Rebecca Snowden Marshall of Baltimore. Miss Marshall states that
the "figure is white wax and the background is a dull red wax,"[2]
that it is approximately 12 by 8 inches, and that she "cannot get
the frame off." It was given to her mother, Mrs. Robert E. Lee
Marshall, as a wedding present on June 6, 1899, by Charles Carroll, governor of Maryland, but its history prior to that is unknown. In the lower left corner appears the inscription "Waugh
Sculpt," though this is not discernible in the photograph.[3]

It is indeed a striking representation in miniature of the tall
figure of the chief justice and supports the Reverend Mr. Hayden's
recollection of the full figure "in the attitude of one delivering a
speech." We can see clearly what Mr. Hayden described as the
"cue," the flapped waistcoat, and the knee breeches. Just when
this version was made and whether there were any others is not
known, but it does appear, as will be pointed out below, that the
wax bas-reliefs by Waugh have been confused with the small
wax busts of Marshall by Robert Ball Hughes.

The records of the Association of the Bar of the City of New
York, in listing objects of art owned by the association, contain an
entry reading: "Marshall, John; wax bust by Ball Hughes, 1829.
Height 7¾". On black pedestal under glass shade. Inscription on
back 'Published as the act directs by Ball Hughes; March 4, 1829.'
(Estate of John L. Cadwalader, 1914.)" But the bust can no
longer be found in the association's rooms, and no record of its
disposition has come to light.[4]

Hughes was born in London and came to America in 1829. He
became an honorary member of the National Academy in 1830
and lived for many years, it is said, in New York City and in
Philadelphia. A sculptor of considerable ability, Hughes himself
proudly stated that while a member of the Royal Academy he
was the "only one of that institution that ever obtained all its
medals."[5] Among the works for which he is remembered in Amer-

2. Rebecca S. Marshall to the author, Nov. 28, 1972.
3. Rebecca S. Marshall to the author, Aug. 20, 1973.
4. Records at the National Portrait Gallery indicate that the bust owned
by the association was the gift of William S. Johnson in 1913, though without evidence of the source of the information.
5. Hughes to Gov. Montford Stokes of North Carolina, Dec. 7, 1831,
quoted in Philipp Fehl, "John Trumbull and Robert Ball Hughes's Restoration of the Statue of Pitt the Elder," *New-York Historical Society Quarterly,*
LVI (1972), 8.

ica are his bas-relief for the tomb of the great Bishop Henry
Hobart in Trinity Church, New York City, the statue of Nathaniel
Bowditch in Mt. Auburn Cemetery in Cambridge, and the statue
of Alexander Hamilton commissioned by New York's Merchants'
Exchange, placed in the Exchange in April 1835 and destroyed by
fire the following December. The latter is known from a wood
engraving published in the New York *Mirror*, October 14, 1835,
and from several plaster representations of it, one owned by the
Museum of the City of New York, another by the Detroit Institute
of Arts.

The inscription reported to be on the wax bust of Marshall
owned by the Association of the Bar of the City of New York in-
dicates that Hughes was protecting his author's interest in his
likeness of Marshall and suggests that there were other copies of
the likeness. Undoubtedly one of these is a wax bust now owned
by the Supreme Court of the United States (fig. 55), given in
November 1961 by Mrs. Miriam E. Wallis of Bala-Cynwyd, Penn-

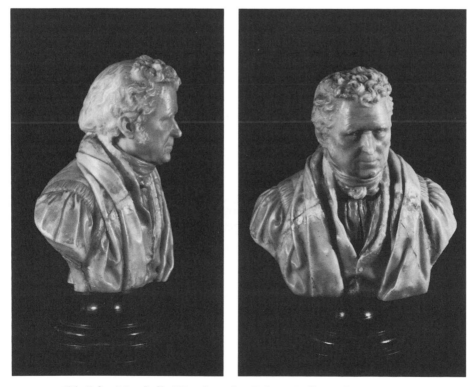

55. John Marshall. Wax bust by Robert Ball Hughes, 1829

sylvania, in memory of her husband. It is approximately 8 inches tall, not including the 7½-inch base on which it stands, and is 7 inches wide at the shoulders. An inscription carved into the back is now only partly legible, all that can be deciphered being ". . . as the Act directs by Ball Hughes . . . 1829." The bust, which shows signs of having been cracked and repaired, stands on the mantel in the Court's East Conference Room below the portrait of Marshall by Rembrandt Peale (fig. 28). Another, comparable in appearance but known only from a photostatic copy of a photograph, belonged a few years ago to Dr. Allen Ludwig of Montclair, New Jersey.

Writing in 1915 about wax portraits, Mrs. Ethel S. Bolton listed nine persons modeled in wax by Ball Hughes, some in several counterparts. Her description of Hughes's wax of Marshall is puzzling: "White wax, full length; knee breeches and old-fashioned long coat; the hair is in a queue; one on a terra cotta background, the one in New York unmounted. The story is that there were six copies of this wax; one has been lost, and one destroyed." This is quite similar to the *Richmond Standard*'s description of the Waugh relief. Mrs. Bolton then lists three of the Hughes examples as then belonging to "Mrs. Charles Marshall, Baltimore," "Mr. Douglas H. Thomas, Baltimore," and "Association of the Bar, New York; unmounted." [6] All of the others she describes are bas-relief likenesses and not busts. In his book on American sculpture, Professor Wayne Craven says of Hughes that "he was the finest modeler of wax profiles in the second quarter of the 19th century anywhere in the country" and "one of the most gifted fashioners of cameo portraits." [7]

Yet there seems to be some confusion about Waugh and Hughes. Waugh's relief is signed, and Hughes's wax bust is inscribed with his name; the authenticity of each is thus firmly established. Mrs. Bolton, however, lists as a Hughes work a profile likeness that must be by Waugh and then an "unmounted" one (which could hardly be a bas-relief) belonging to the Association of the Bar of the City of New York, which at one time did own a bust by Hughes. Without seeing the other examples listed by Mrs. Bolton, we cannot conclusively solve the problem. The

---

6. Ethel Stanwood Bolton, *Wax Portraits and Silhouettes* (Boston, 1915), 73. The terra-cotta background referred to by Mrs. Bolton is probably what Miss Rebecca Marshall describes as "dull red wax."

7. Wayne Craven, *Sculpture in America* (New York, 1968), 30.

only thing that can be said with certainty is that Waugh made at least two bas-reliefs of Marshall (figs. 53 and 54) and that Hughes made several small wax busts (fig. 55), including those belonging at one time to the bar association and to Dr. Ludwig. Both of these types are splendid portraits of the chief justice.

Chapter 14

Robert Matthew Sully
(1803–1855)

W OLVES," so says tradition, "first took gold to Delphi." [1]
Robert M. Sully, so says tradition, painted four portraits of John Marshall. But six have been found, each
with some evidence of having been painted by Sully.

Robert Sully, a nephew of the great portraitist Thomas Sully,
was born in Petersburg, Virginia, in 1803. The son of an actor
with a taste for drawing who died when his son was scarcely ten
years old, Robert took to painting at the age of sixteen. A year or
so later he visited Philadelphia, where he was able to study under
his uncle. Of that experience he wrote: "My obligations to my
uncle I shall ever remember with gratitude. I remained with him
eight or nine months, and on my return to Virginia commenced
professionally. 'A prophet hath no honour in his own country.' I
soon found that a painter is generally equally unfortunate in the
city of his residence." [2] Sully then studied a while in England,
where he was permitted to exhibit at the Royal Academy. In 1829
he was home again, working in Philadelphia, and later in Richmond and Washington. He died in Buffalo, New York, in 1855 on
his way west to make his home in Wisconsin.

At least six portraits by or attributable to Sully are known, and
the problem is to sort them out. The Virginia Constitutional Convention, held during the winter of 1829–1830, offered to painters
an opportunity to catch the likenesses, in some cases the last portraits from life, of some of the early participants in the founding
of the young Republic. Sully, like others, took advantage of the
occasion and painted, among other great men, the chief justice.
Marshall's opinion of Sully is amiably expressed in a letter of introduction the chief justice wrote in 1830 to his friend John
Vaughan of Philadelphia, at one time secretary of the American
Philosophical Society: "Mr. Sully a young artist of merit is desirous of trying his fortune on a larger theatre than our village,

1. Fredrika Bremer, *Greece and the Greeks*, trans. Mary Howitt (London, 1863), II, 153.
2. William Dunlap, *History of the Rise and Progress of the Arts of Design in the United States* (New York, 1834), II, 153.

and desires me to introduce him to some gentleman whose partiality for the arts and general character in Philadelphia may furnish the inclination and ability to give him that countenance, information, and may I say advice which a young man among strangers always needs. I hope not to oppress you with any real inconvenience when I take the liberty of presenting him to you as a person who will not disgrace your recommendation." [3]

Over the years some confusion has arisen as to just when Sully painted Marshall and which of the several portraits is the first. Let us examine the evidence.

In 1854, twenty-five years or so after the event, Sully wrote to the first secretary of the State Historical Society of Wisconsin: "I have, in my time, painted three different portraits of Chief Justice Marshall. One is in our *City Hall,* another in the Court House, at Staunton, Va., the 3rd in possession of a private family, this last I think I will be allowed to copy, if so, I will present it to your Society." [4] Hanging in the city council chamber of the old City Hall in Richmond in 1972 was a handsome portrait of Marshall (fig. 56), approximately 43 by 32½ inches in size, not in very good condition and perhaps overcleaned. It was then about to be moved to the new City Hall, the nearby rooms already being stripped of their furnishings. When the portrait was last cleaned, the records show that it was signed "R. M. Sully 1829," though the signature was not apparent when I saw the portrait in 1972. A newspaper account of the portrait in 1951 confuses the issue: "Little was known about the portrait of Chief Justice John Marshall until it was cleaned recently. But it is signed by R. M. Sully, 1829, and the Valentine Museum has records showing that Sully painted Marshall at least three times. One of these is in the Corcoran Museum in Washington, and a second belongs to the Wisconsin Historical Society. No one knows when the city obtained its copy or under what circumstances." [5] No one, that is, who had not read the minutes of the Richmond City Council meetings. The minutes of the meeting of Monday, November 9, 1835, reveal the

3. Sept. 10, 1830, reproduced in facsimile in William H. Brown's *Portrait Gallery of Distinguished American Citizens, with Biographical Sketches, and Fac-similes of Original Letters* (Hartford, Conn., 1845), opposite the silhouette of Marshall by Brown (fig. 67) at the commencement of the volume, the page being unnumbered.

4. Sully to Lyman C. Draper, May 13, 1854, State Historical Society of Wisconsin, Madison.

5. *Times-Dispatch* (Richmond), Aug. 29, 1951, 4.

56. John Marshall. Oil by Robert Matthew Sully, 1829

following: "Committee appointed to procure a full-length likeness of Chief Justice John Marshall and suspend in a suitable frame in City Hall. Members of Committee–James E. Heath, William Mitchell, and John S. Myers." [6] The committee not having made much headway, the meeting of June 18, 1836, replaced members Myers and Mitchell with Gustavus A. Myers and John A. Lancaster. On January 10, 1837, success was achieved, with the committee reporting:

That they have for the sum of two hundred and fifty dollars, procured a half-length portrait of their late illustrious fellow citizen, John Marshall, remarkable, as they think, for the fidelity of its resemblance to the original and highly creditable as a specimen of the native talent. Your Committee cannot but felicitate themselves, that in performing the duty required of them by the resolution of the Common Council, they have also been enabled to encourage the talents of the artist–Robert M. Sully, Esqr., a native and citizen of Richmond. Resolved that the Chamberlain be authorized to permit to Mr. Robert M. Sully, to have the use of the portrait of the late Chief Justice Marshall for the purpose of making a copy thereof. [7]

The minutes are at best vague, if not ambiguous. Was the portrait that the Council received a posthumous portrait, or was it one that Sully had painted from life and kept himself? The likeness is so strong and the portrait exhibits such depth and dignity that I have no doubt that it is a life portrait and that we can rely on its signature and date. It has none of the flat, shallow, characterless appearance so often encountered in a copy or imaginary likeness; it portrays Marshall in all the vigor and dignified self-possession he exhibits in the other great life portraits, such as Inman's (fig. 73).

There has recently been found a small drawing (fig. 57) that is very likely the preliminary sketch for the 1829 portrait (fig. 56). The sketch is on paper in what appears to be brown ink over pencil, 12 by 7¾ inches in size, and now belongs to Victor Spark of New York. In the lower right-hand corner it bears an inscription, "Drawn from life & Presented to A. Placide, Sketch of Judge Marshall, R. M. Sully, April 1, 1832." The date might well be the date of gift to Placide. The general pose, the strong rendering of the hands, the close facial similarity between the sketch and por-

6. Richmond City Council Minutes, Council Book 10, 127, Virginia State Library, Richmond.
    7. *Ibid.*, 226.

trait, and particularly the presence of what appears to be the spine of a large volume near Marshall's left shoulder, an incidental feature but one that appears in both sketch and portrait, all conspire to suggest strongly that the drawing was preliminary to the portrait. It would be quite natural that the finished painting would be reduced to three-quarter length and the informal cross-legged pose eliminated. It is of interest to note in the sketch Marshall's invariable custom of wearing knee breeches rather than long trousers. The identity of A. Placide has escaped us; perhaps he was related to Henry Placide, a popular actor of the day.

But now what of the copy Sully was to make, for which he borrowed the Richmond City Council's portrait? He himself listed as his second portrait of Marshall one in the Circuit Courthouse at Staunton, Virginia, and a replica of the 1829 portrait is there, but in such poor condition that it is difficult to judge its merit. It is somewhat larger than the original, 52 by 42 inches. According to an article in the *Staunton Spectator* of May 11, 1837, the portrait was commissioned by prominent citizens of Staunton. The artist received $300 for the portrait, including its frame, and accompanied the portrait to Staunton in June 1838 to supervise its hanging in a good light. This would seem to dispose of two of the three portraits Sully mentioned to Draper. What of the last named, that "in possession of a private family"?

We have a record of a third Sully, but it is quite a different likeness of Marshall, so different that it is hard to believe it was painted in 1829 or 1830 during the Virginia Constitutional Convention. To discover its origin we have to jump ahead, late in Sully's life.

The State Historical Society of Wisconsin, chartered in 1853, had as its first secretary Lyman C. Draper, a believer in publicity who "missed no opportunity to advertise himself, the Historical Society, the city of Madison and the State of Wisconsin." [8] In 1854 Draper procured as a gift from Thomas Sully a copy of his portrait of George Washington and through Sully got in touch with his nephew Robert. The younger Sully agreed to make a copy of his portrait of the Indian chief Black Hawk, which was in the possession of the Virginia Historical Society, and of two other portraits he had painted, one of Black Hawk's son and another of White Cloud, all for the sum of $100. The money was raised and

8. William B. Hesseltine, *Pioneer's Mission: The Story of Lyman Copeland Draper* (Madison, Wis., 1954), 146.

57. John Marshall. Ink and pencil on paper by Robert Matthew Sully, 1829

sent to the artist, and he, in grateful appreciation, agreed to send to the society "as a free gift a copy of his portrait of Marshall, painted from life, in the Virginia Historical Society." [9]

In March 1855, Sully wrote to Draper: "You will be gratified to learn that I can now Positively Promise a Portrait of *Judge Marshall*. After great difficulty, it is (the original) in my actual Possession. The Proprietor having very kindly lent it, for the purpose of making a copy, a Favour that would not have been granted to any one else. I congratulate you on this! as you will have an excellent likeness of a great & what is better a good man. The last of the Mohicans." On April 15 he continued: "I have now really good news to tell you. Look out soon for the Portrait of Marshall, it is *half finished,* and I give you my word, it will be the best portrait I ever painted. The original was painted twenty or more years ago, in my *spring time.*" Again on June 26: "Your Marshall, is now nearly done, I have only to Robe his Judgeship, and it will be complete." At last on August 25 he wrote: "Now for good news, tomorrow I varnish *Judge Marshall,* & the Society will *really* have a good Picture. I was careful in not having it much seen, for fear the Society here, might wish a copy, which I have neither time nor desire to execute. A relation of the family did see it and observed (I give you his own words) 'that such a Picture should not leave Virginia. That must be Purchased &c.' To which I quickly responded, that the Picture was the property of the Wisconsin Hist. Sy. under such circumstances it *could not* be purchased. Now, mind, I will at once box him up, & send him, as I did the others." [10]

"Send him" he did and was then promptly elected an honorary member of the society. The whole affair so pleased and interested him that he decided to move out to Wisconsin to live. He set out from Richmond but died en route at Buffalo, New York, on October 16, 1855.

The Wisconsin Historical Society's portrait (fig. 58), 36 by 29 inches, is not signed but bears on the reverse: "Chief Justice Marshall / Painted by R. M. Sully / Presented by RMS / to the Histl. Society of / Wisconsin / Richmond Va / 1855." Stenciled

9. Louise Phelps Kellogg, "Pocahontas and Jamestown," *Wisconsin Magazine of History,* XXV (1941–1942), 39, 42.

10. Extracts from Letters from Robert Sully to Lyman Draper, State Hist. Soc. of Wis.

58. John Marshall. Oil by Robert Matthew Sully, 1855

on the back appears "From / W. S. Attler / 141 Main St. / Richmond, Va.," presumably the framer or shipper.

Where is the so-called "original" from which Sully made this
copy? An article in the *Wisconsin Magazine of History*, quoted
above, stated that the portrait was copied from a "portrait of
Marshall, painted from life, in the Virginia Historical Society."
But Sully in May 1854 told Draper of only three portraits he had
by then painted of Marshall, one at the Richmond City Hall, its
copy at Staunton, and a third "in possession of a private family."
In the course of making the copy he had written that "the Proprietor" of the portrait had kindly lent it and that he didn't want
it seen lest "the Society here might wish a copy." "The Society
here" presumably meant the Virginia Historical Society. It is
safe to assume, therefore, that in 1854 the "original" was in fact in
private hands and that the 1942 reference in the *Wisconsin Magazine of History* was in error. Curiously enough, the records of
the Virginia Historical Society indicate that on February 4, 1857,
Thomas H. Ellis of Richmond gave a portrait of Marshall to the
society, but it cannot be firmly established whether it was a
portrait by Sully or by Cephas Thompson. The society at one time
had portraits of Marshall by both artists, but during the evacua-
tion of Richmond in 1865 they were removed by friends of the
society and placed for safekeeping in the vaults of a Richmond
bank, a well-intentioned effort but with an unhappy ending. The
bank was destroyed when Richmond was burned, and both portraits were lost. Perhaps the lost Sully owned by Ellis was the one
copied for the Wisconsin Historical Society.

The Corcoran Gallery of Art in Washington has a similar portrait (fig. 59), 37 by 29¼ inches in size. In 1900 John Sidney
Webb wrote from Washington to Professor James B. Thayer of
the Harvard Law School: "In regard to the portrait by Sully in
the Corcoran Gallery of Art, the record is that it was received
July 20, 1887, from G. W. Mayo of Richmond, Virginia, and is
supposed to have been painted about 1843." [11] In a recent catalog
of American paintings in the Corcoran Gallery it is stated that
this portrait has on the back of the canvas "L. G. Allan / 1830,"
that it came from the collection of Mrs. Louisa G. Allan of Richmond by purchase in 1887, and that it "is one of three painted by
Robert Sully in Richmond during the Virginia Constitutional

11. Dec. 27, 1900, Thayer Papers, Harvard University Law School,
Cambridge, Mass.

59. John Marshall. Oil by Robert Matthew Sully, 1830

60. John Marshall. Oil by an unknown artist, attributed to
Robert Matthew Sully, 1829–1830

Convention in 1829/30, the other two being in the City Hall of
Richmond and in the Court House at Staunton, Virginia." [12] The
Corcoran portrait, therefore, can also lay claim to being the
"original" copied by Sully for the Wisconsin Historical Society. It
has all the appearances of an original life portrait, while the Wisconsin picture looks less like one and by no means justifies Sully's
claim that it would be the "best portrait" he ever painted.

But there is one more claim to be considered. In the Virginia
Museum of Fine Arts there hangs a fine portrait of the chief
justice (fig. 60), received in 1935 as a gift from John Barton

12. *A Catalogue of the Collection of American Paintings in the Corcoran
Gallery of Art* (Washington, D.C., 1966), I, 64.

Payne, the records at the time apparently indicating that the artist was unknown. But we have an interesting clue to its origin. The picture is reproduced as the frontispiece to the second volume of John F. Dillon's *John Marshall: Life, Character and Judicial Services*, where it is also described in detail in a quotation from a letter that the then owner of the portrait, Judge John Barton Payne of Chicago, wrote to Dillon in 1901:

Chief Justice Marshall was a member of the Virginia Constitutional Convention of 1829–30. While in Richmond attending the Convention a committee of that body engaged R. M. Sully to paint his portrait, the plan being to present the portrait to the Convention and through it to the State of Virginia. The portrait was not finished when the Convention adjourned and it remained the property of the artist, and it, together with a portrait of the elder Booth, descended to Mrs. Cole, wife of the Rector of the Episcopal Church at Culpepper Court House, Virginia. After the assassination of President Lincoln the Federal troops slashed the Booth portrait with their sabres and destroyed it. The Marshall portrait was undisturbed and remained in the Cole family at Culpepper until 1891, when it was acquired by me through T. Willoughby Cole of that family, now a resident of Chicago. Conway Robinson, of Virginia, who knew Chief Justice Marshall personally, pronounced this portrait the best likeness of Marshall known. The Sully portrait was exhibited at the World's Fair, Chicago, in 1893; at the Atlanta Exposition, and at the Art Institute in Chicago.[13]

There is the evidence that has so far come to light; there may well be more. It is unlikely that Sully forgot one or two replicas he had painted over the years, but it is not impossible. If he still had in his possession the portrait described by Judge Payne (fig. 60), then why would he have troubled to spend the spring of 1855 copying another portrait borrowed from its "Proprietor" —or was the whole thing a trick he was playing? But memories often play us false. In his seventy-third year John Quincy Adams made a list purporting to comprise all the portraits that had by then been painted of him; yet in fact he omitted some and included others that had not been done.[14] I believe that figure 56, following its preliminary sketch, figure 57, is the original Sully portrait of Marshall, later reproduced in the portrait for the Staunton courthouse. Of the second type of Sully likeness, I strongly suspect that figure 60 is the original, that Judge Payne

13. John F. Dillon, comp. and ed., *John Marshall: Life, Character and Judicial Services* . . . (Chicago, 1903).
14. Oliver, *Portraits of John Quincy Adams*, 2.

fell into error in describing part of its early history, and that figure 59 is an early replica of figure 60. Figure 58 is, of course, the replica done years later for the Wisconsin Historical Society, probably taken from figure 60. We have to make a judgment objectively as art historians on the evidence that is available. Tradition is unreliable. "Wolves," so says tradition, "first took gold to Delphi."

Chapter 15

George Catlin
(1796–1872)

CATLIN was one of those artists privileged to be present in the winter of 1829–1830 at Virginia's Constitutional Convention, at which were gathered together for the last time so many of the historic figures of the early days of the Republic that the convention became known as "the last meeting of the giants."[1] Like all gatherings it attracted not only the general public but also artists, as in our time photographers and television networks, to perpetuate the occasion and preserve for future generations the likenesses of those present.

The *Richmond Compiler* of October 23, 1829, disclosed that "Mr. Catlin from New York has taken rooms for portrait and Miniature Painting at Mrs. Duval's Boarding House."[2] Catlin is best known, of course, for his likenesses of Western Indians, now coveted by collectors of Americana. His presence in Richmond in 1829 was prompted by a hope not only of professional employment but also of a climate better suited to his poor health than that of Albany, New York, where he had lately been active in painting portraits of prominent persons of that city.

It has been said, without convincing evidence, that Catlin was called to Richmond and commissioned to paint a picture of the convention. The roster of famous Americans in Richmond for the occasion was impressive—ex-Presidents Madison and Monroe, Chief Justice Marshall, Governor William R. Giles, John Randolph of Roanoke, to name but a few of the ninety-six delegates. Here was the opportunity of a lifetime for an enterprising portraitist; in addition to Catlin, Chester Harding and Robert M. Sully were there. Like many an artist before and after him, Catlin was entranced with the dream of painting such a distinguished group as a body, with true likenesses of all the delegates. John Trumbull's dream had come true by the end of the eighteenth

1. R. W. C. Vail, "The Last Meeting of the Giants," *New-York Historical Society Quarterly*, XXXII (1948), 69–77.

2. Quoted in "Catlin's Virginia Convention of 1829–1830," Virginia Historical Society, *An Occasional Bulletin*, No. 23 (Oct. 1971), 11.

century with his *Declaration of Independence*. Samuel F. B. Morse was to do the same in 1821 with his great picture of the *Old House of Representatives* (fig. 23). Such pictures could be reproduced by copperplate engravings, from which prints might be, it was believed, readily sold by subscription if not to the public at large.

Catlin advertised his scheme in the *Richmond Compiler* on December 15, 1829. Hugh Blair Grigsby of Norfolk, the youngest delegate present, decided that Catlin "was not only an artist of great worth, but a man of good taste in letters," and determined to assist him "in the fulfillment of his designs." From the Virginia Historical Society's *Occasional Bulletin* of October 1971, we learn that Grigsby many years later wrote to Robert C. Winthrop of Boston, recalling that he had introduced Catlin "to the Members [of the Convention] whom I brought to his studio, and had the pleasure of seeing his work fairly completed." [3] To further his design Catlin himself invited the delegates "to call . . . at my painting Rooms at Mrs. Duval's and allow me to make a sketch of your heads for my picture of the Convention." [4]

The finished picture shows the convention at its opening when James Madison addressed the chairman, James Monroe. Marshall is shown seated almost directly behind Madison. The occasion has been stirringly described by Chester Harding, who was present at that historic moment: "It was a noble sight to behold the first step in the proceedings of that body. They, as you know, chose Mr. Monroe as the president. It was truly affecting to all present, when, after the unanimous voice of the Convention had proclaimed him their head, the Chief Justice and Mr. Madison led him to the chair. The stillness of death pervaded the whole house, which was only broken by the tremulous voice of the president. Insignificant as this Convention was in comparison with that of Seventy-six, it nevertheless brought that illustrious body to my imagination very forcibly. Indeed, this trio of revolutionary veterans seemed almost a part of that august assemblage." [5]

We are told that Catlin made first a watercolor sketch, 21⅝ by 32⅞ inches in size, which showed in detail the interior of the old House of Delegates chamber in Richmond and included all the delegates and visitors in their places as they appeared at the

3. *Ibid.*   4. *Ibid.*
5. Harding to S. F. Lyman, Feb. 25, 1830, quoted in Margaret E. White, ed., *A Sketch of Chester Harding, Artist—Drawn by His Own Hand* (Boston, 1890), 199.

Convention (fig. 61). Not unlike the way Trumbull had painted his *Declaration of Independence,* Catlin painted one by one the likenesses of all the individuals who were present. Whether they were painted directly onto the sketch or done separately and added later is conjectural—perhaps both methods were used. The likenesses, each about one inch in size, included the ninety-six delegates, the chaplain, editors of the two leading Richmond papers (the *Whig* and the *Enquirer*), and the clerk and the stenographer of the convention. As was observed in the *Occasional Bulletin:* "An irreverant biographer has concluded that 'Catlin made that august convention a crowded parliament of gnomes with huge heads and warped dwarfed bodies.'" [6] Nevertheless, many of these miniature likenesses are the only surviving portraits of those particular delegates. Others are recognizable likenesses when compared with contemporary portraits by other artists. Marshall, Madison, and Monroe are unmistakable, if not good, likenesses.

But Catlin's task was not an easy one. In the midst of his endeavors his wife became very ill. Dolley Madison, then in Richmond, on hearing that there was a stranger in town who was sick and in need of help, came to her aid and nursed her so that Catlin could get his sketch finished before the convention adjourned. With understandable gratitude Catlin repaid her the only way he could, by painting a charming miniature of her on ivory. On completing the watercolor sketch (fig. 61) Catlin made a pen and ink key (fig. 62) of approximately the same size, in which he identified all the figures. The key also contains two notes in Catlin's hand not readily legible to the naked eye, each indicating that Catlin apparently intended the key to be engraved in its final form. The note at the top of the sketch reads: "This key is not to be engraved, as a more careful one will be prepared and engraved in this Country. George Catlin. Richmond, Va. 1830." The note at the foot of the sketch, between the rows of seats reads: "There is a fault in the drawing—occasioned by Carelessness, by making this Seat [at this point a hand is drawn in, pointing to the right] lower than the one on the lefthand, which the Engraver will please to correct."

Catlin then copied the picture in oil on a walnut panel approxi-

6. Va. Hist. Soc., *An Occasional Bulletin,* No. 23 (Oct. 1971), quoting Loyd Haberly, *Pursuit of the Horizon: A Life of George Catlin, Painter & Recorder of the American Indian* (New York, 1948), 342.

61. The Virginia Constitutional Convention of 1829–1830. Watercolor sketch by George Catlin, 1829–1830

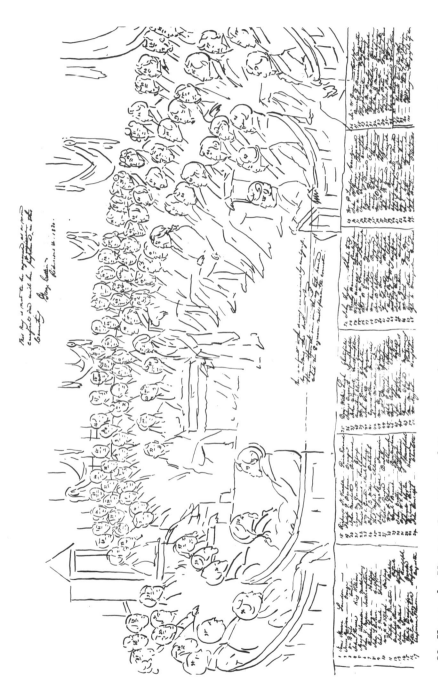

62. Key to the Virginia Constitutional Convention of 1829–1830. Pen and ink on paper by George Catlin, 1830

mately 24 by 36 inches (fig. 63), but from that point on, the original and the copy had a different history.[7]

In 1831 Catlin tried to persuade the Virginia General Assembly in Richmond to purchase the oil painting (fig. 63) for the Commonwealth of Virginia, his petition stating that the painting would "be exhibited for a few days at my Painting Rooms at the Eagle Hotel, where the members of the Legislature are anxiously invited to examine and judge of its merits." But if they "examined," they were clearly unable to "judge" and declined to take advantage of the opportunity to acquire the picture, thereby unwittingly setting a precedent that the Congress (also unwittingly) followed when in 1846 it failed to acquire Gilbert Stuart's portraits of the first five presidents and when in 1897 it similarly passed over John H. I. Browere's collection of twenty-two busts of great Americans.

Catlin found the watercolor and the key also impossible to sell or to reproduce by engraving on satisfactory terms; so he took them with him to Europe with his collection of paintings and sketches of American Indians and there exhibited them from 1839 to 1852. It has been said that he sent an india-ink copy of the sketch of the convention to Lafayette for reproduction in Paris but that it was "overlooked and neglected." Such a copy has not come to light. Becoming involved in financial difficulties, in 1852 Catlin borrowed money from the Philadelphian Joseph Harrison, Jr., on the security of the watercolor and its key (figs. 61 and 62) and some of the Indian paintings that he had with him. He died in 1872, never having had the ability to pay off the loan and redeem the paintings. In 1870 he had deposited another part of his collection with the New-York Historical Society and had tried to sell it and what was in Harrison's hands to the society, guaranteeing delivery of the pledged paintings even though by then Harrison claimed he had bought them in 1852. The society did buy some two hundred Catlin drawings, but the watercolor and the key remained in Harrison's possession. Until 1879 they were stored in the damp, often water-soaked rooms of Harrison's boiler factory. Then the Smithsonian Institution acquired from Harrison's heirs most of the paintings but not the sketch and the key or the oil painting of the convention. In 1885

7. For details see Va. Hist. Soc., *An Occasional Bulletin*, (Oct. 1971), and Vail's "Last Meeting of the Giants," *N.-Y. Hist. Soc. Qtly.*, XXXII (1948), 69–77.

63. The Virginia Constitutional Convention of 1829–1830. Oil on panel by George Catlin, 1830

the former were "in the possession of a Philadelphia gentleman," [8] who was in fact Thomas C. Donaldson, to whom the Harrison heirs had given them. In October 1947 the New-York Historical Society, their present owner, acquired the sketch and the key through a dealer from Donaldson's son Thomas B. Donaldson.

At some point, however, the oil panel (fig. 63) was separated from the watercolor sketch, and nothing is known of its whereabouts from 1830 to 1888, when it was sent to Boston from England by the antiquary Benjamin F. Stevens, who believed it represented a Massachusetts convention. It was quickly identified and sent on to Richmond in another vain attempt to persuade the Commonwealth to purchase it. St. George T. C. Bryan finally bought it, even though he did not know that a key existed and could identify only a few of the persons represented. Later, believing he had made a bad bargain, he sold the oil at a loss to Thomas W. Winston, a client of John Hart's. Hart, a Richmond dealer, then tried to dispose of it and deposited it in 1932 with Alexander W. Weddell in Virginia House in Richmond, where it remained in Weddell's possession until his tragic death in a train wreck in 1948. Meanwhile Hart had died, and the Virginia Historical Society learned of the purchase of the key by the New-York Historical Society. Weddell's executors thought that he had owned the panel but were in a quandary after becoming aware of a conflicting claim that Winston, through Hart as his agent, had purchased it about 1907. They deposited the panel for safekeeping with the Virginia Historical Society. After eight years of negotiation a settlement was finally effected with Winston's widow, and the panel is now safely lodged with the society as its owner.

Although Catlin is best known for his magnificent series of paintings of American Indians, nevertheless his two sketches of the "last meeting of the giants" are priceless historical documents and would alone have given him a place among those who have preserved on canvas the important events of the early days of the Republic.

8. Thomas C. Donaldson, *The George Catlin Indian Gallery in the U.S. National Museum (Smithsonian Institution) with Memoir and Statistics* (Washington, D.C., 1886), 707.

Chapter 16

William Henry Brown
(1808–1883)

THE "LAST OF THE SILHOUETTISTS," as William H. Brown was called, was born in Charleston, South Carolina. After an early start at his craft, he became one of America's foremost silhouettists. He cut from sight and also from memory, and in many instances superimposed his profiles on stereotype interior or landscape backgrounds that were lithographed for him by E. B. and E. C. Kellogg of Hartford, Connecticut. Between 1820 and 1835 he cut most of his better-known likenesses, the most famous group of which was copyrighted in 1845 or 1846 as part of the Kelloggs' volume *Portrait Gallery of Distinguished American Citizens,* where they were reproduced in lithograph facsimile. Unfortunately, almost the entire edition was destroyed by fire, and copies are today rare and valuable. In 1931 a reprint was published, which is the familiar volume known to many of us.[1]

Brown's interest and skill went beyond the simple portrait profile. His second book, *The History of the First Locomotives in America* (New York, 1871), showed the extent of his ability. The old capitol building in Hartford still exhibits an extraordinary seven-foot silhouette representation of the "De Witt Clinton," the Mohawk and Hudson Railroad train that first ran between Albany and New York, August 9, 1831.

Among his portrait silhouettes, Brown highly esteemed the Marshall likeness. Before even opening the Kellogg volume, we find on the front cover in gold stamping the figure of the chief justice seated in a chair holding an open book on his knee (fig. 64). The same likeness is reproduced on the cover of the 1931 reprint. The medium, die stamping on a cloth cover, is such that the figure is somewhat crude and primitive in appearance. What is believed to be the original pen and ink silhouette from which the cover illustration was taken is still in existence and belongs

1. William H. Brown, *Portrait Gallery of Distinguished American Citizens, with Biographical Sketches, and Fac-similes of Original Letters* (New York, 1931 [orig. publ. Hartford, Conn., 1845]).

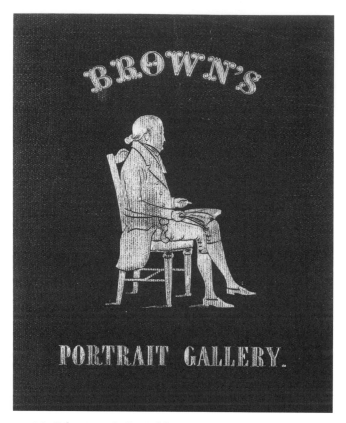

64. John Marshall. Gold stamping on book, 1845

to the Massachusetts Historical Society (fig. 65). It is a good profile likeness of Marshall and shows him as he invariably dressed, in knee breeches. On the back of the sketch is written: "Portrait of Chief Justice Marshall / Drawn from the original picture and presented to the / Mass. Hist. Soc. by Charles Brown Esq. of Boston / September 26, 1839"; and beneath it, in a different hand, the added words: "From this the engravings have been taken."

The whereabouts of "the original picture" are not known, but the Massachusetts Historical Society has another version of the same likeness (fig. 66) that might qualify for the original. It was given to the society on October 19, 1967, by Mrs. Mark DeWolfe Howe among a small album of engravings and silhouettes collected by Eliza Susan Quincy, daughter of Josiah Quincy, the sixteenth president of Harvard. Written on the back of it appears:

65. John Marshall. Silhouette on paper by William H. Brown, *ca.* 1831

66. John Marshall. Silhouette on paper by William H. Brown, date unknown

"Chief Justice Marshall, being found in the desk of Joseph Story and presented to me by his widow—Oct. 1845." This silhouette was reproduced with modifications in Charles Henry Hart, "Last of the Silhouettists," *Outlook*, LXVI (Sept.–Dec. 1900), 329, and also in the 1926 edition of Josiah Quincy, *Figures of the Past*, opposite page 202.[2] These must have been the "engravings" referred to in the note on the back of figure 65.

Let us now open the Kelloggs' volume of lithographed silhouettes. There, as the first of the twenty-six lithographs (after the frontispiece of Washington) is a full-length silhouette of Marshall (fig. 67), superimposed on one of the Kelloggs' backgrounds. Marshall makes a fine figure, tall, upright, vigorous, and lifelike. The lithograph, 13⅜ by 9⅞ inches, is inscribed: "From life by Wm. H. Brown—Lith. of E. B. & E. C. Kellogg / John Marshall / Entered according to act of Congress in the year 1844 by E. B. & E. C. Kellogg, in the Clerk's office of the District Court of Connecticut."

Other versions of the standing figure are known, some undoubtedly replicas done by Brown, others just copies. In 1917 a standing silhouette belonged to Douglas H. Thomas of Baltimore, who gave a photograph of it to the Boston Athenaeum. It was signed "W. H. Brown" in the lower right-hand corner and is a modification of the lithograph, or perhaps the source of it. Still another version is the familiar silhouette showing both Marshall and the aged, bent figure of Richard Channing Moore (fig. 68), owned by the Virginia Historical Society. It could be a replica by Brown or a copy, but it bears no inscription. Despite a slightly different pose and treatment of the hat, the profile of Marshall is clearly traceable to the lithograph type. There are several others almost indistinguishable. It was a popular representation of the old gentleman.

The Virginia Historical Society has an additional silhouette of Marshall (fig. 69), 13 by 10 inches, showing the judge with hat in hand. It bears his autograph and, at the foot, an inscription partly obliterated by a tear: "[Silhou]ette from life by Brown, cut in 1830—the original in the possession of James Evans Esqr. Richmond, Va." It is not known when, or in whose hand, the inscription was added. The writer seemingly did not know

2. Josiah Quincy, *Figures of the Past, from the Leaves of Old Journals* . . . (1883), new ed. with introduction and notes by M. A. DeWolfe Howe (Boston, 1926).

From life by Wm.H.Brown.   Lith. of E.B.& E.C.Kellogg.

JOHN MARSHALL.

Entered according to act of Congress in the year 1844 by E.B.& E.C.Kellogg, in the Clerks office of the District Court of Connecticut.

67. John Marshall. Lithograph silhouette after William H. Brown, 1844

68. John Marshall and Bishop Richard Channing Moore. Silhouettes on
paper, that of Marshall by or after William H. Brown

Brown's first name or initials and left a blank space to be filled in
later. This likeness was listed in *Portraiture in the Virginia Historical Society* and reproduced in the April 1901 issue of the
Green Bag.[3]

In the aggregate these shadows give us a fine view of the old
chief justice as he appeared in 1830, aged seventy-five, at about
the time he was painted by Catlin (fig. 61), Sully (fig. 56), and
Harding (fig. 44), and a year before Inman's great portrait (fig.
73). Except for Harding's monumental portrait (fig. 44) and
Beverley Waugh's wax representation (fig. 54), Brown's is the

3. Alexander Wilbourne Weddell, *Portraiture in the Virginia Historical
Society* (Richmond, 1945), 122; *The Green Bag: An Entertaining Magazine for Lawyers,* XIII (1901), 181.

ette from life by   Brown, cut in 1880. the original in the possession of James Evans
Esq: Richmond, Va.

69. John Marshall. Silhouette by William H. Brown, 1830

only full-length view of Marshall from life that remains, and it adds a new dimension to our gallery of likenesses.

Auguste Edouart, the great French silhouettist who cut thousands of silhouettes during his sojourn in this country in the decade from 1839 to 1849, copied Brown's standing silhouette. His copy (fig. 70) was included in one of the few volumes of his works that survived his shipwreck when he returned to France on the *Oneida* in 1849. The volume contains over three hundred silhouettes of prominent Americans, and undoubtedly Edouart felt that such a gathering would not be complete without a view of Marshall. The volume now belongs to a private collector in Pennsylvania.

Brown's seated view of the chief justice was influential in the design of the statue of Marshall by William Wetmore Story that now stands on the west side of the Capitol in Washington. Story, an able sculptor, was the son of Marshall's long-time associate Justice Joseph Story. The day after Marshall's death the Philadelphia bar recommended to the national bar a cooperative effort to erect a monument in Washington to the memory of the great chief justice. On August 10, 1835, a circular letter went out seeking contributions not to exceed $10 each. As can be imagined, insufficient funds were raised. The proceeds of the appeal, $4,000, were held by trustees, of whom William T. Wilbank of Philadelphia was the leader, as the "Marshall Memorial Fund." By 1882, forty-seven years later, the fund had grown to $20,000. Just as the bar was about to reconsider the plan, Congress stepped in with legislation:

Be it enacted by the Senate and House of Representatives of the United States of America Assembled, That the President of the Senate and the Speaker of the House of Representatives do appoint a joint committee of three Senators and three Representatives with authority to contract for and erect a statue to the memory of Chief Justice John Marshall, formerly of the Supreme Court of the United States; that said statue shall be placed in a suitable public reservation, to be designated by said joint committee, in the city of Washington, and for said purpose the sum of twenty thousand dollars, or so much thereof as may be necessary, is hereby appropriated, out of any money in the Treasury not otherwise appropriated.[4]

On December 21, the government signed a contract with Story for a statue of the chief justice with an appropriate pedestal.

4. U.S., *Statutes at Large*, XXIII, 28; approved Mar. 10, 1882.

70. John Marshall. Silhouette by Auguste Edouart, *ca.* 1840

71. John Marshall. Bronze statue by William Wetmore Story, 1882–1884

Story set to work. The statue and pedestal were modeled and cast in Italy and arrived in New York in two huge cases by the steamer *Elyria* from Rome in April 1884. There was a certain amount of confusion because Story had directed delivery to the librarian of Congress, Ainsworth R. Spofford, rather than to the "United States." After some rather heated correspondence, the collector of the port of New York was instructed to admit the cases free of duty, and at last they reached Washington. Story's efforts met with general satisfaction. On May 10, 1884, with appropriate ceremony, in the presence of some two score of Marshall relatives, the "Noble Statue," as the press referred to it (fig. 71), was dedicated, with Chief Justice Morrison R. Waite

72. John Marshall. Bronze statue by William Wetmore Story

presiding and William H. Rawle of Philadelphia delivering the address.[5]

At that point on May 12, 1884, the librarian wrote to the secretary of the Treasury, the Honorable Charles I. Folger, advising him of the receipt of the statue and asking him to "please cause a warrant to issue and a Draft on the Ass't Treasurer at New York to be mailed direct" to Story at his address, Palazzo Barberini, Rome.[6]

For some years there was a question about what Marshall was holding in his left hand, some believing it was intended to represent the Constitution. The matter was laid to rest to everyone's

5. Charles E. Fairman, *Art and Artists of the Capitol of the United States of America* (Washington, D.C., 1927), 487–488.

6. Ainsworth R. Spofford to Folger, May 12, 1884, Letterbook No. 12 (1883–1888), Archives, Library of Congress.

satisfaction by Joseph Warren of Washington—it was intended to be "an opinion of the Chief Justice." [7]

Appearing on the sides of the pedestal are allegorical figures, Minerva, Philosophy, Jurisprudence, Commerce, and Education, with Victory laying a spear on the altar of the Union to which she leads young America to swear allegiance. Religion, pointing upward, stands on the side of the altar; nearby is an Indian musing over the meaning of allegiance and peace and over the changes that have turned his hunting grounds into farms and cities.

A counterpart (fig. 72), on a different form of pedestal, belongs to the Pennsylvania Museum of Art and stands in Fairmount Park in Philadelphia.

But the inspiration for these large statues was Brown's small three-inch silhouette, taken fifty years before.

7. Joseph Warren to James B. Thayer, Mar. 25, 1901, Thayer Papers, Harvard University Law School, Cambridge, Mass.

Chapter 17

Henry Inman
(1801–1846)

HENRY INMAN'S great portrait of Marshall (fig. 73), painted in October 1831, has always occasioned high praise of both the artist and his subject. Professor James B. Thayer of the Harvard Law School said: "The portrait is regarded as the best that was ever taken of him in his later life. Certainly it best answers the description of him by an English traveler, who saw him in the spring of 1835, and said that 'the venerable dignity of his appearance would not suffer in comparison with that of the most respected and distinguished-looking peer in the British House of Lords.' " Mr. Justice James T. Mitchell of the Supreme Court of Pennsylvania said, "There are many portraits of the Chief Justice, but most of them by inferior artists who failed wholly to catch or portray the spirit and character of the man." Inman's portrait, in contrast, "gives us the mature man, with all the qualities that his contemporaries ascribe to him—the thin, rather small face, the broad brow with a mass of dark hair growing low down on it, the benign half smile, and the keen but kindly black eyes that William Wirt said 'possess an irradiating spirit which proclaims the imperial powers of the mind within.' "[1]

It was an attack of the stone that brought Marshall to Philadelphia late in September 1831 to consult Dr. Philip Syng Physick, the aged and distinguished surgeon. Consultations were held, examinations conducted, and the dreaded operation was agreed upon and scheduled for mid-October. Meanwhile the chief justice's presence in Philadelphia did not go unnoticed. At a meeting of the bar of the city on September 30 there were strong expressions of admiration for Marshall. At an adjourned meeting the next day the following resolution was adopted:

Resolved, That the Chairman of this meeting [William Rawle, chancellor of the Law Association of Philadelphia] be requested to wait on

1. Both Thayer and Mitchell are quoted in John F. Dillon, comp. and ed., *John Marshall: Life, Character and Judicial Services* (Chicago, 1903), III, iv.

73. John Marshall. Oil by Henry Inman, 1831

Chief Justice Marshall and express to him the request of the Bar of Philadelphia, that he will permit his portrait to be taken.

Resolved, That a committee be appointed to obtain the services of an eminent artist of this city to carry into execution the purpose of the foregoing resolution, should Chief Justice Marshall, assent thereunto.

Resolved, That these proceedings be published.[2]

Marshall graciously consented to sit, notwithstanding the precarious state of his health and the ordeal that hung over him.

On October 6 he wrote to his wife: "My dearest Polly: Today I am to receive a very flattering address from the young men of the City which will I ardently hope be the last."[3] The operation was set for October 13, but the heavy rains kept Dr. Physick at home. Marshall wrote to his wife on October 12: "Cary Ambler called on me yesterday and left his card. I am sorry that I had stepped to the office of a portrait painter who is employed by the gentlemen of the bar to take my portrait. I did wrong to go out, but could not resist the desire to comply with their request. The Doctor has laid his interdict on my going out again."[4] A few days later the operation was performed, successfully. Dr. Jacob Randolph, who assisted in the operation, gives a splendid account of the fortitude and resignation of the seventy-six-year-old chief justice and the skill of Dr. Physick.

He [Dr. Physick] felt somewhat reluctant to operate upon Chief Justice Marshall, and offered to place the case in my hands. Taking all the circumstances into consideration, and knowing well that this would be the last time he would ever perform a similar operation, I felt desirous that he should finish with so distinguished an individual; and accordingly urged him to do it himself. Upon the day appointed, the Doctor performed the operation with his usual skill and dexterity. I do not think I ever saw him display greater neatness than on that occasion. The result of the operation was a complete success.

It will be readily admitted that, in consequence of Judge Marshall's very advanced age, the hazard attending the operation, however skilfully performed, was considerably severe. I consider it but an act of justice, due to the memory of that great and good man, to state, that in my opinion, his recovery was in a great degree owing to his extraordinary self possession, and to the calm and philosophical views

2. Samuel Hazard, ed., *Hazard's Register of Pennsylvania. Devoted to the Preservation of Facts and Documents, and Every Kind of Useful Information,* VIII (1831), 237–238.

3. Marshall Papers, Swem Library, College of William and Mary, Williamsburg, Va.

4. *Ibid.*

which he took of his case and the various circumstances attending it.

It fell to my lot to make the necessary preparations. In the discharge of this duty I visited him in the morning of the day fixed on for the operation, two hours previously to that at which it was to be performed. Upon entering his room I found him engaged in eating his breakfast. He received me with a pleasant smile upon his countenance, and said, "Well, Doctor, you find me taking breakfast, and I assure you I have had a good one. I thought it very probable that this might be my last chance, and therefore I was determined to enjoy it and eat heartily." I expressed the great pleasure which I felt at seeing him so cheerful, and said I hoped all would soon be happily over. He replied to this, that he did not feel the least anxiety or uneasiness respecting the operation or its result. He said that he had not the slightest desire to live, labouring under the sufferings to which he was then subjected; that he was perfectly ready to take all the chances of an operation, and he knew there were many against him; and that if he could be relieved by it he was willing to live out his appointed time, but if not, would rather die than hold existence accompanied with the pain and misery which he then endured.

After he had finished his breakfast, I administered to him some medicine; he then inquired at what hour the operation would be performed. I mentioned the hour of eleven. He said, "Very well; do you wish me now for any other purpose, or may I lie down and go to sleep?" I was a good deal surprised at this question, but told him that if he could sleep it would be very desirable. He immediately placed himself upon the bed and fell into a profound sleep, and continued so until I was obliged to rouse him in order to undergo the operation.

He exhibited the same fortitude, scarcely uttering a murmur, throughout the whole procedure, which from the peculiar nature of his complaint, was necessarily tedious.[5]

This is a touching description of the grand old man whose likeness Inman has preserved for us, taken only a day or so before. At his recovery everyone rejoiced.

On November 17 the young members of the bar of Philadelphia wrote: "As Philadelphians we think ourselves entitled to be proud, that SCIENCE has *here* wrought what we shall have the approbation of our countrymen in calling an inestimable benefit to the nation."[6] Convalescence was slow, but in December, Marshall sent a vase to Dr. Physick inscribed "This tribute

5. Jacob Randolph, *A Memoir on the Life and Character of Philip Syng Physick, M.D.* (Philadelphia, 1839), 97–99.
6. *Niles' Weekly Register*, XLI (1831), 259.

of gratitude for restored health is offered by J. Marshall." But his blessings were not unmixed. On Christmas day his wife of almost forty-eight years, his "dearest Polly," died, and he was left to recover his health and carry on alone. How well and bravely he did so is recorded elsewhere.[7]

But what of the portrait? It is signed "Chief Justice Marshall / Painted by Henry Inman, 1832. / Original." Yet there was a lithograph reproduction of it, 12¾₆ by 10⅟₆ inches, made by the deaf mute lithographer Albert Newsam, which bears these inscriptions: "Painted by H. Inman," "From the original portrait painted by order of the Bar of Philadelphia," and "Entered according to act of Congress, in the year 1831, by Childs & Inman in the Clerk's office of the District Court of the Eastern District of Philadelphia."[8] Cephas G. Childs and Henry Inman were partners at this time and employed Newsam as their principal lithographer of portraits. The difference in the dates of the lithograph and the signed portrait can be attributed to the fact that Newsam had the opportunity to make his lithograph before the actual completion of the portrait whereas Inman presumably didn't sign and date it until it was actually completed. The portrait today belongs to the Philadelphia Bar Association but is on loan to the Department of State, Washington, D.C. In 1832 it was exhibited at the Pennsylvania Academy of the Fine Arts, and in 1846 it was shown, with many others of Inman's portraits, at the Art-Union Rooms at 322 Broadway, New York, for the benefit of his widow and family. "Admittance" to the latter exhibition was "25 Cts," and the catalog sold for "12½ Cts," with the Marshall portrait listed as number 10.

The high quality of the painting and the striking likeness of the great and beloved chief justice required, as can be imagined, frequent reproductions, of all sorts and by many different artists.

James B. Longacre and James Herring were among the first to seek reproduction for their *National Portrait Gallery of Distinguished Americans*,[9] employing Asher B. Durand for the purpose. Durand, who had established his reputation as an engraver by

7. See, for example, Albert J. Beveridge, *The Life of John Marshall* (Boston, 1916–1919), IV, chap. 10.

8. D. MacN. Stauffer, "Lithograph Portraits of Albert Newsam," *Pennsylvania Magazine of History and Biography*, XXIV (1900), 435.

9. James B. Longacre and James Herring, *The National Portrait Gallery of Distinguished Americans* (Philadelphia, 1834–1839). A facsimile reprint edition was published in 1970.

his magnificent 1823 engraving of Trumbull's *Declaration of In-dependence,* wrote to Inman for access to the portrait for the purpose of engraving it. Inman replied in July 1832: "I have just recd. yr. favour of the 30th ulto. and in reply have to state that the original portrait of Marshall is at present in the Phila. Academy. I can get it in a week hence and will incontinently proceed to copy it. You shall have it in a month hence at farthest. I am glad you are to do it. I should not permit it to go into any body else's hands." [10] This is an odd statement in view of the fact that it had already been lithographed by Newsam. But what it does establish is that Durand's engraving was taken from the replica (fig. 74) and not from the original, as comparison will show. Durand's engraving is inscribed, "Eng. by A. B. Durand / John Marshall LLD. / J. Marshall (auto) / Entered according to the act of Congress in the year 1833 by James Herring in the clerk's office of the District / Court of the Southern District of New York." Justice Joseph Story wrote a sketch of Marshall for the *National Portrait Gallery* and received a grateful letter from Marshall dated July 31, 1833: "I have received the 3d No. of the National Portrait Gallery and know not in what terms to express my obligations to you for the more than justice you have done the character of your brother Judge." [11]

After Durand had used the replica for making his engraving, it was bought by Marshall and given to his daughter, Mary. Years later, in 1885, George D. Fisher of Richmond, Virginia, corre-sponded with the Boston lawbook seller Charles C. Soule about likenesses of Marshall suitable for reproduction in quantity. A great admirer of Marshall's, Fisher in his youth had known the famous jurist and was enthusiastic about the project. He also knew Mrs. Ellen Ruffin, Marshall's eldest granddaughter, whom he consulted. Fisher quoted to Soule what Mrs. Ruffin had told him: "The picture in the Capitol [at Richmond] was taken in Philadelphia by 'Inman' in 1831, he being at that time 76 years of age. Uncle Edward [Coke Marshall] preferred that, to any other likeness of my Grandfather, and repeatedly advised persons who wished portraits of him, to see that one. We value it par-ticularly, because he had it taken for my Mother, and I miss it

10. H. Inman to A. B. Durand, July 2, 1832, A. B. Durand Papers, New York Public Library, New York City. This letter was brought to my atten-tion by David B. Lawall, curator of the Bayly Museum, University of Vir-ginia, Charlottesville.

11. Story Papers, Harvard University Law School, Cambridge, Mass.

74. John Marshall. Oil by Henry Inman, 1832

so much, that I often wish for the means to have a copy taken for the place it now stands in, so that we could have this again, over our parlor mantel piece." Fisher's letter continued: "I need only add by way of confirmation, of the good painted portrait by 'Inman' now hanging in the gallery of our Capitol, that Mrs. Ruffin's Uncle Edward C. Marshall, (now dead) was the youngest son of the Chief Justice, and was born the same year as myself, 1804, and died about 5 years ago—so his opinion of that portrait, I value more highly than my own." [12]

The portrait descended from Marshall's daughter to two of her daughters, the Misses Ann F. and Emily Harvie, Ellen Ruffin's sisters. Recognizing the significance of the portrait, they deposited it on loan with the Virginia State Library—and on the death of the survivor of the sisters, Emily Harvie, in January 1920, it was found that the portrait had been bequeathed to the Commonwealth of Virginia. For years it hung in the capitol in Richmond "among a large number of conspicuous men of War, Governors, etc.," [13] but it has recently been placed on loan to the Jamestown Foundation at the Jamestown Festival Park near Williamsburg, where it has apparently been parted from its frame.

A comparison of Durand's engraving (fig. 75) with figures 73 and 74 will make it apparent that figure 74 is the replica that Durand and Inman corresponded about in July 1832. For example, note the identical folds on Marshall's right shoulder and sleeve in figures 74 and 75 as compared with those in figure 73.

The number of copies, engravings, and other reproductions of the Inman portrait of Marshall is legion, but they all seem to stem from one of these three: the original, the replica, or Durand's engraving. Reproducing or listing all would hardly be justified and could scarcely hope to be complete, but it seems worthwhile to take into account some of those that have known histories or that have appeared or hang in prominent places.

The Historical Society of Pennsylvania owns a portrait of Marshall of the Inman type painted by Jacob Eichholtz (fig. 76). The portrait appears to have been copied from figure 73; note the shape of the folds of Marshall's right shoulder and sleeve and the treatment of the stock. Consider also that Eichholtz was painting in Philadelphia, where the original Inman portrait of

12. Fisher to Soule, Aug. 19, 1885, Letters of George D. Fisher relating to John Marshall, University of Virginia Library, Charlottesville.
13. Fisher to Soule, July 17, 1885, *ibid.*

75. John Marshall. Engraving by Asher B. Durand, 1833

76. John Marshall. Oil by Jacob Eichholtz, 1841

Marshall was. He would not have had as ready access to the replica (fig. 74) in Richmond. On the back of the canvas is written, "This portrait of the late / Judge Marshall is / presented to the Colonization / Compy of Philadelphia by / J. Eichholtz 1841." The American Colonization Society presented it to the Historical Society of Pennsylvania on July 20, 1923. Eichholtz was born in Lancaster, Pennsylvania, in 1776, studied under Gilbert Stuart in Boston in 1812, was a regular exhibitor at the Pennsylvania Academy from 1823 until his death in 1842, and spent most of his career in Lancaster and Philadelphia. The American Colonization Society was organized in Washington in 1817 "to promote and execute a plan for colonizing (with their consent) the Free People of Colour residing in our country, in Africa, or such other place as Congress shall deem it most expedient." [14] The society's first president was George Washington's slaveholding nephew Justice Bushrod Washington. In 1818 Marshall was listed as having become a life member of the society

14. Stated purposes, quoted by Francis Russell in *The American Heritage History of the Making of the Nation* (New York, 1968), 160.

77. John Marshall. Oil by Jacob Eichholtz, *ca.* 1841

78. John Marshall. Oil by William B. Chambers

"upon the payment of $30," which he sent to Bushrod Washington on June 17, 1819.[15] Separate societies were formed in several states, and in 1831 John Marshall was chairman of the Virginia Colonization Society. Presumably Marshall's interest in the colonization program prompted Eichholtz to present his portrait to the Pennsylvania Colonization Society.[16]

Another copy by Eichholtz (fig. 77), without showing Marshall's hand or the book on his knee, is owned by The Brook, in New York City. It was purchased for The Brook by Mr. C. X. Harris in 1913 from Miss Angelice K. Smith of Intercourse, Pennsylvania, a granddaughter of the artist. At that time Mr. Harris was told by Miss Susie L. Ziegler of Lancaster, Pennsylvania (a stepdaughter of the artist's son Robert), that the artist's daughter

15. Miscellaneous Manuscripts, New-York Historical Society, New York City.

16. Marshall's interest in colonization is also shown in an 1831 petition to the Virginia House of Delegates, Accession No. 9431, Virginia State Library, Richmond.

Elizabeth had told her mother that she distinctly remembered her father going to Virginia to paint the portrait.[17] It is, however, unlikely that Eichholtz would have gone to Virginia to copy the replica when the original was at hand in Philadelphia. The recollection may well have been based on wishful thinking that the painting was an original life portrait. It is, in any event, a fine copy of Inman's original and, in turn, is believed to be what William B. Chambers followed when he painted the small portrait (fig. 78) formerly owned by the American Scenic and Historic Preservation Society and now owned by the New York State Office of Parks and Recreation. This portrait came to view in the Ehrich Galleries early in this century and was then acquired by Alexander S. Cochrane and given by him in 1929 to the Preservation Society. Nothing more of its provenance is known.

From 1825 to 1863 Daniel Wesley Middleton served as assistant clerk and then clerk of the Supreme Court of the United States. He had therefore known and served under four chief justices: Marshall, Roger B. Taney, Salmon P. Chase, and Morrison R. Waite. He collected a portrait of each of these justices and hung the paintings in his home as a memorial and reminder of the great jurists under whom he had served. His portrait of Marshall (fig. 79) is a copy or, it is remotely possible, even a replica of the original Inman (fig. 73). After Middleton's death the portraits were offered for sale, and a bill was introduced in Congress recommending their purchase for $8,000. The Senate's Committee on the Library of Congress, to whom the bill was referred, reported in part as follows:

It appears that the Secretary of the Treasury, out of all the portraits of John Marshall now extant, selected this one to be engraved in steel at the Bureau of Engraving and Printing for use as a vignette upon Government bonds and notes, and as such it may now be seen upon the face of the twenty-dollars Treasury note, upon the face of the $1,000 4 per cent Government bond, issue of 1895, and also upon the disbursing officers' check of the Department of Justice.

This portrait of Marshall is probably a copy, made during the jurist's lifetime, of the great painting by Henry Inman, which is in the law library of Philadelphia, or a replica by the artist himself. This opinion is sustained by the eminent engraver, Mr. John Sartain, who wrote the following letter after viewing the Government engraving made

17. This account appears in Diego Suarez, *The Collection of Portraits of American Celebrities and Other Paintings Belonging to The Brook* (New York, 1962), 8, in which "Eichholtz" is spelled throughout "Eichlotz."

79. John Marshall. Oil by an unknown artist

80. John Marshall. Engraving by Charles Schlecht, before 1890

81. John Marshall. Oil by an unknown artist

82. John Marshall. Oil by an unknown artist

from the portrait now on sale, and making careful comparison and study of its lines and the modeling of the face with those of steel engravings of the authenticated Inman portraits:

"My impression is that the print of Judge Marshall that you have is copied (engraved) from a duplicate picture of the one Henry Inman painted from life, and is now in the law library of Philadelphia (or used to be). The original of your print may be a replica by Inman himself or a copy by some good painter."[18]

Despite the favorable recommendation of its library committee, Congress did not appropriate the money to buy the four portraits. A further attempt made in 1909 and 1910 also failed, at which point the Honorable Frank B. Brandagee, senator from Connecticut, purchased the portraits and presented them to the State of Connecticut. They are now in the Connecticut State Library in Hartford. The portrait of Marshall is a good reproduction of Inman's likeness, and it is hard to add much to what Sartain said of it. The "Government engraving" (fig. 80), taken from the portrait owned by Middleton, was executed by the engraver Charles Schlecht and is of a lower order of excellence. Variations of this made by the American Banknote Company appear on the five-dollar ordinary postage stamps, Series of 1894 and 1902.

There are in Richmond a group of portraits after the Inman likeness probably taken from the readily available replica (fig. 74), which hung so long in the Virginia State Library. One (fig. 81) hung in 1972 in the chambers of the United States District Court Judge Robert R. Merhige, Jr., in the old Post Office building. The artist is unknown, and no information as to its source was available. Another (fig. 82) of which nothing is known hangs in the John Marshall Hotel at Fifth and Franklin streets, Richmond, Virginia, and is the source of the likeness that decorated the tag attached to the hotel's room keys. When the tag was discontinued, a few were encased in lucite and used as souvenirs, shown here as figure 83.

Hanging in the John Marshall House in Richmond is a copy (fig. 84) made in 1915 by Mrs. Jeffrey G. A. Montague, a popular portrait painter active in Virginia from 1900 to 1920. Mrs. Kenneth R. Higgins, a Marshall descendant, owns a copy (fig. 85) done by John Slavin in 1932. Slavin was a well-known Richmond

18. State of Connecticut, *Report of the State Librarian to the Governor* (1911–1912), 26–27.

artist who died in 1971 and had presumably copied the replica (fig. 74). The Virginia Historical Society has an early copy (fig. 86), given to it in 1857 by the artist, William Barksdale Meyers, who was then only seventeen years old. As the society's president wrote in 1945, "Certainly it is a work of promise for one so young." [19]

In 1844 George Peter Alexander Healy received a commission from Louis Philippe, king of France, to paint for him a series of portraits of great Americans. Healy was able to capture life portraits of John Quincy Adams, Jackson, and Clay, and copied

83. John Marshall. Key tag set in lucite

portraits of deceased presidents and of Marshall (fig. 87). It is not known which version of Inman he followed, but the portrait found its way to France, hung for awhile in the Historical Gallery at Versailles with the king's collection of American worthies, and is now in the Musée de la Coopération Franco-Américaine, in the Chateau de Blérancourt, Aisne, France.

George C. Lambdin, the eldest son of James Reid Lambdin, many years ago copied an Inman likeness, which was deposited

19. Alexander Wilbourne Weddell, *Portraiture in the Virginia Historical Society* (Richmond, 1945), 72.

84. John Marshall. Oil by Mrs. Jeffrey
G. A. Montague, 1915

85. John Marshall. Oil by John D. Slavin,
1932

86. John Marshall. Oil by William Barksdale Meyers, 1857

87. John Marshall. Oil by George Peter
Alexander Healy, *ca.* 1845

with the Maryland Historical Society on loan in 1886 and later bequeathed to the society by the late Mrs. J. V. McNeil. The portrait (fig. 88) is a poor copy and only remotely resembles Marshall.

James Reid Lambdin, on the other hand, painted several copies presumably after the Inman original, which was close at hand in Philadelphia. Lambdin, born in Pittsburgh, had studied under Sully and had become a well-known portrait painter, an officer of the Pennsylvania Academy, and an honorary member of the National Academy. He sold one of his portraits of Marshall to the Union League of Philadelphia on September 25, 1867, at the time the league acquired a number of Lambdin's Civil War portraits. The portrait was restored and repaired in 1972 by Joseph Amartico at the Pennsylvania Academy of the Fine Arts and is illustrated here as it appeared after the restoration (fig. 89). Another copy, now attributed to Lambdin (fig. 90), was acquired from the late Thomas B. Clarke by Andrew Mellon and given to the National Gallery of Art. Later it was transferred to the National Portrait Gallery. It is not as good a copy as the one owned by the Union League, and there is, of course, no positive proof that Lambdin painted it, though it has long been attributed to him.[20]

So much for J. R. Lambdin's copies after Inman. We have some evidence, however, that Lambdin painted a life portrait of Marshall. His daughter Emma C. Lambdin copied her father's journal, portions of which have been published. One section of her copy has the following entry, not otherwise supported:

Early in January 1832 I again visited Washington to paint a portrait, of Chief Justice Marshall. . . . He was boarding with the other members of the Supreme Bench at Tench Ringolds, near the White House. The venerable Chief received me with great kindness and courtesy, and cheerfully complied with the request that he should sit to me, but, said the only time that he could give me would be before breakfast. "If," he said, "you can be here by 7 o'clock in the morning I will sit to you 'till 8." This arrangement was agreed upon. I was punctual and

20. See Theodore Bolton, "A Catalogue of the Paintings of Henry Inman," *Art Quarterly*, III, supplement (1940), 409, in which Bolton quotes from a letter from William Sawitzky, Dec. 30, 1932: "Who painted the copy in the Thomas B. Clarke collection I don't know, but I am convinced it was not Lambdin, who was a much better painter. It is inferior to any other copy I have ever seen." Sawitzky had presumably not seen the copy at the Maryland Historical Society (fig. 88).

88. John Marshall. Oil by George C. Lambdin, *ca.* 1867

89. John Marshall. Oil by James Rei᳇ Lambdin, 1867

90. John Marshall. Oil attributed to James Reid Lambdin, date unknown

91. John Marshall. Oil by an unknown artist, *ca.* 1840

from time to time had as many sitting's as I desired. The portrait was deemed entirely satisfactory to him and his friends.[21]

This quotation has been applied to figure 90, but that portrait could not be independent of the Inman likeness. We are forced to the conclusion that Lambdin's life portrait, if it existed at all, is presently unlocated.

One early and puzzling portrait of Marshall is that acquired by the Stanford School of Law in 1966 from the late Philip L. Roe of Baltimore (fig. 91). Turning first to the back of the portrait, we find two handwritten inscriptions. The earlier one reads: "This painting of the Superior Judge of the Court of the United States was painted by the painter Robert Edge Pine. The property of Daniel Bowen, Boston." The later inscription follows: "The painting of Judge John Marshall was restored by me at the request of Mr. Daniel Bowen. Please do not restore again. Joseph Stain." Following the word "Stain" the paper is torn, and the letters "er" appear on a piece of paper inserted in the blank— perhaps the end of the word "restorer," which might have been on the next line. There is some evidence that when the painting was last restored, "the restorer changed the jabot on the painting —it was a frilly jabot, rather than the plain stock always worn by Marshall. It has been overpainted in—probably by the first restorer of the painting, Joseph Stain."[22]

If it had not been for the inscriptions on the back, this portrait perhaps would never have been considered to be a representation of Marshall. But there they are. Stain was a restorer of paintings and a framer who worked in Boston in the 1840s. Bowen, born in 1760, maintained a series of wax museums and art collections in Boston and prided himself on his collection of paintings by Robert Edge Pine. Pine, however, died in 1788 when Marshall was but thirty-three years old and hardly a likely subject for a portrait—certainly not a portrait of a middle-aged man. The name of Pine must therefore be attributed to Bowen's optimism or advertising acumen. No likely artist presents himself, but there is just enough similarity to the Inman portrait to suggest that this might be a copy—perhaps a copy of some presently unknown

21. Corcoran Gallery of Art, *Loan Exhibition of Portraits of the Signers and Deputies to the Convention of 1787* . . . (Washington, D.C., 1937), 90.

22. Report on the portrait by Jean L. Finch, art librarian, Stanford University School of Law, Stanford, Calif., in the author's files.

reverse engraving. Failing that, we fall back on the not impossible circumstances that the labels (despite Bowen's hopes) referred to some other portrait. There it is: provenance unknown, one label clearly wrong, the other questionable, but a lingering chance that the portrait owned by Stanford could be an early and poor copy of a derivative of the great Inman likeness.

The Marshall-Wythe School of Law at the College of William and Mary has a copy (fig. 92) of the Inman portrait by an unknown artist, presented by Miss Agnes Robinson of Washington, D.C. It is a modern copy and though a likeness, not an attractive one.

In July 1899 the artist George K. Knapp presented his copy of Inman's Marshall to the city of Philadelphia for Independence Hall. The portrait (fig. 93) is inscribed in the lower left-hand corner, "G. K. Knapp 1899 after H. Inman 1833." It is not a particularly good copy but requires notice because of the number of people who see it at Independence Hall.

The Pennsylvania Academy of the Fine Arts also possesses a portrait of Marshall after Inman (fig. 94), the origins of which are unclear. In the academy's archives there is a document, dated November 1, 1831, relating to an effort to obtain a portrait of Marshall: "The Subscribers . . . being desirous of testifying their respect for John Marshall . . . hereby agree to contribute the sum of Five Dollars each in order to procure a full length portrait of him by Mr. Inman, to be presented to the Penna. Academy of the Fine Arts for permanent exhibit in that institution." [23] The statement was signed only by H. D. Gilpin, W. Gratz, George Harrison, and later by eight others. But nothing came of the proposal. The portrait now owned by the academy (fig. 94) was received on April 12, 1933, with many other portraits from the John Frederick Lewis Collection and was exhibited in the Lewis memorial exhibition in 1934. The academy's file relating to the painting contains a receipt for an "oil portrait" for $1,005 running to "M. Jackson" from Samuel T. Freeman and Company, auctioneers of Philadelphia, dated December 4, 1913. A note in the same hand and apparently the same ink reads, "Deliver to Penna. Academy of Fine Arts, Broad and Cherry Sts." In a different hand and ink appears, "Portrait of John Marshall by Henry Inman. . . . From Sale of Edward S. Willing," and in a third

23. Quoted in a letter to the author from Susan W. Cooley of the Pennsylvania Academy of the Fine Arts, Philadelphia, Nov. 11, 1971.

John Marshall. Oil by an unknown artist, *ca.* 1840

93. John Marshall. Oil by George H. Knapp, 1899

John Marshall. Oil by an unknown artist

95. John Marshall. Oil by Eliphalet F. Andrews, 1891

hand, "John F. Lewis." A newspaper clipping dated "December 1913," also in the file, describes the sale of "furniture and fittings of the home of the late J. R. Barton Willing," including "a portrait of Chief Justice Marshall," which "brought $1005 at the second day's auction sale." According to the clipping, the Marshall likeness "was a replica of the portrait by Henry Inman, an early American artist, which adorns the walls of the Law Library in City Hall." [24]

The academy has no record of any such painting being delivered in 1913, nor was the painting illustrated by figure 94 in its collections until 1933. It may be, therefore, that the portrait sold at Freeman's and the portrait received from the Lewis Collection are not the same picture. The Lewis Collection portrait, however, is an able reproduction of the Inman likeness but with very scant provenance.

In 1939 a portrait then attributed to Inman (and clearly a copy or replica of the Inman original) was owned by Mrs. Leonard K. Elmhurst of New York and England. It was reproduced in *Life in America: A Special Loan Exhibition of Paintings Held during the Period of the New York World's Fair* . . . (New York, 1939), 50, illustration 71. This catalog was printed in an edition of ten thousand copies. The portrait has since dropped from sight.

Eliphalet F. Andrews, an able artist who in the 1880s and 1890s painted copies of well-known portraits for various government buildings, copied one of the Inman portraits in 1891 (fig. 95). The painting was purchased by the Department of State from the artist on November 25, 1891, for $100, a reasonable price for a good copy in those days. [25] It was later reproduced in Richard S. Patterson, *The Secretaries of State: Portraits and Biographical Sketches* (Washington, D.C., 1956), 10.

When Professor James B. Thayer was preparing his memorial account of Marshall for the centennial of his appointment as chief justice, his daughter desired to copy the Inman portrait, which was then hanging in the Philadelphia Bar Association law library in Philadelphia. Francis Rawle, one of the leading members of the Philadelphia bar, wrote to Thayer: "Fortunately the Library Committee held its monthly meeting today and placed the portrait at your disposal. You will receive more formal notice, but need not wait for it. Two rooms with excellent light are hardly

24. *Ibid.*
25. Records of the National Portrait Gallery, Washington, D.C.

ever used. The picture can be placed there. I beg you will let us
know when Miss Thayer is coming. I will arrange to go with her
and have the picture so placed as to suit her wishes." [26] The formal
notice came a month later from the librarian: "I reported to the
Library Committee your desire as to a copy of the Inman Marshall portrait, and they complied with much pleasure, and desired
me to accord your daughter such facilities as the Library can
command. . . . Your daughter can be given a very pleasant
room connected with the Library, warm, airy & bright, where
she will be undisturbed." [27] Miss Theodora W. Thayer went
straight to work and completed her copy in short order. On
May 18, 1901, John H. Arnold, librarian of the Harvard Law
School, acknowledged, in the name of "the President and fellows
of Harvard College, . . . a copy of the Inman Portrait of Chief
Justice John Marshall. By Miss Theodora W. Thayer. A gift to
the Law Library of the University from James B. Thayer and
[his son] Ezra B. Thayer Esq.," for which they returned "grateful
acknowledgment." [28] The grateful acknowledgment, however,
was part of the standard, printed receipt form, to which the gift
and the donors' names were added. At this late date we must not
doubt the gratitude of the president and fellows, but the portrait
cannot be found.

The Inman likeness is unquestionably the most popular and
has been more often reproduced in engravings and woodcuts
than any other. A few examples will illustrate the range covered
by such reproduction. One of the earliest (fig. 96) is a proof of
the woodcut that appeared in 1839 in the *American Magazine.*[29]
It appears to have been taken from the Inman original, but by
whom is not known. In 1853 John W. Orr of New York engraved
a Marshall after Inman (fig. 97) for A. D. Jones's *Illustrated
American Biography*, the engraving bearing the initials "S. W."
under Marshall's right side.[30] No clue to "S. W." has been found.
Orr himself was a well-known engraver much in demand as a
book and magazine illustrator.

26. Jan. 12, 1901, Thayer Papers, Harvard University Law School, Cambridge, Mass.

27. Luther E. Hewitt to J. B. Thayer, Feb. 9, 1901, *ibid.*

28. Arnold to J. B. Thayer and Ezra R. Thayer, May 18, 1901, *ibid.*

29. *American Magazine of Useful and Enlivening Knowledge*, III
(1839), 133.

30. A. D. Jones, *The Illustrated American Biography, Containing Correct
Portraits and Brief Notices of the Principal Actors in American History* . . .
(New York, 1853–1855), I, 183.

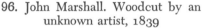

96. John Marshall. Woodcut by an   97. John Marshall. Wood engraving
    unknown artist, 1839   by John W. Orr, 1853

For the first volume of Frank Moore's *American Eloquence,*
published in 1857, William G. Jackman engraved a small likeness
after Inman (fig. 98), which appeared in several states. Jackman,
born in England, worked principally in New York for book pub-
lishers. Thomas B. Welch's small vignette of Marshall (fig. 99)
appeared in 1836, on the title page of *The American Orator's
Own Book,* a sort of orator's miniature *vade mecum.*[31]

In 1935 the late Thomas Blakeman of North Truro, Massachusetts, made an etching and aquatint of Marshall after Inman (fig.
100), his notes indicating that he "finished the head with dry
point and gravure." [32] It was made and reproduced in some quantity to be framed and hung, and copies are in the Library of
Congress, Harvard, Princeton, and Duke universities, the Association of the Bar of the City of New York, and the Minneapolis
Museum of Art. Blakeman didn't follow Inman closely, and the
result bears some resemblance to the Lambdin copy in the Maryland Historical Society (fig. 88). It is not known which portrait
Blakeman used.

A poor likeness, in the form of a miniature vignette, done by

31. *The American Orator's Own Book, or the Art of Extemporaneous
Public Speaking* . . . (Philadelphia, 1836).
32. Mrs. T. B. Blakeman to the author, June 4, 1972.

98. John Marshall. Engraving by
William G. Jackman, *ca.* 1857

99. John Marshall. Engraving by Thomas
B. Welch, 1836

100. John Marshall. Etching, aquatint, and
drypoint by Thomas Blakeman, 1935

John Rogers, is among the engravings appearing in figure 101. No clue to the source of this illustration has been found, and it is an interesting subject for speculation as to what textual matter could be illustrated by engraved "likenesses" of Gilbert Stuart, Robert Morris, Samuel Adams, John Marshall, and Thomas Paine. The illustration appears to be a page from a book published in New York by Virtue and Company.

One of the most acceptable derivatives from Inman's original portrait of Marshall is the monumental posthumous portrait painted by William D. Washington for the Fauquier County Courthouse in Warrenton, Virginia (fig. 102). The large painting, which hangs behind the bench, is approximately 109 by 63 inches in size and is signed in the lower right-hand corner, "W. D. Washington / Washington," and a few letters that could be either a date or "B. C." [33] It was mentioned by Marshall's granddaughters Ann F. and Emily Harvie in a note enclosed in a 1901 letter from Justice Horace Gray to Professor James B. Thayer, which says that "the portrait in Warrenton was in a manner a copy of the one in the Library," that is, of Inman's replica (fig. 74) deposited by the Misses Harvie in the Virginia State Library in Richmond.

Washington was paid $500 for painting the portrait, and the completed work was duly accepted by an order of the court dated June 27, 1859. Here is an account of how it survived the Civil War:

There now hangs over the Judge's seat in the handsome court room in Warrenton, a splendid lifesize painting considered one of the best in existence, of John Marshall, the great chief justice of the United States. It is in a very heavy gilt frame. It was painted, framed and hung in the court house many years before the war at the expense of the county and was regarded with the greatest veneration. When the war began and the armies began to go back and forth and battles were fought all around, and violence was rampant, the prominent people of Warrenton became fearful that the painting would be destroyed or stolen. The county was not deemed a safe place for it so it was cut from its frame, rolled and enclosed in a tin case, and at the instigation of Mr. Charles Kemper sent to Mr. Theo. Kemper in Cincinnati, and stood in a fireproof vault in his office during all the long years of the War. At its close Mr. Theo. Kemper returned the

33. Washington's portrait is described in the *Fauquier Historical Society Bulletin*, 1st Ser. (1929–1934), 143–144.

101. John Marshall and others. Engraving by John Rogers

102. John Marshall. Oil by William D. Washington, 1859

103. John Marshall. Detail from oil by Richard N. Brooke,
1881

painting to its friends in Warrenton, and it now hangs again in its
frame and place in the court room, the pride of the county.[34]

A copy of Washington's portrait was sought for the Capitol,
and in 1880 Richard N. Brooke was commissioned by the Library
Committee of Congress to execute one (fig. 103). It was purchased from him in 1881 and now hangs in the west corridor of
the House wing, third floor. In the lower right-hand corner is the
signature "R. N. Brooke / Washington 1880." The portrait is reproduced in Charles E. Fairman's *Art and Artists of the Capitol
of the United States of America* (Washington, D.C., 1927), 463.
Brooke had another opportunity to display his interest in this
likeness of Marshall. In 1889, at the time of the election of Grover
Cleveland as president of the United States, the Warrenton Courthouse burned, and W. D. Washington's portrait of Marshall is

34. Willis Miller Kemper, *Genealogy of the Fishback Family in America* . . . (New York, 1914), 68.

104. John Marshall. Oil by David Silvette, 1946

said to have been saved by being cut out of its frame by Brooke.

Another copy was sought by the University of Virginia for its law school in the 1940s. The account of the effort and its result is told in an article by Robert B. Graham, Jr., in the November 19, 1971, issue of the *Virginia Law Weekly*. The article recounted the beginning of the effort to obtain a portrait in 1941 and stated, in part:

Shortly after World War II, Dean [F. D. G.] Ribble and Professor William A. White renewed the campaign. Through Edmund S. Campbell of the University Art Department, they arranged for Artist David Silvette to copy an existing portrait. Mr. Silvette suggested the one which hung in the Warrenton, Va., Court House. . . . Already copied once by Richard Norris Brooke for the United States Capitol, the painting was approved by Dean Ribble for the University.

Mr. Silvette offered his services at pre-war prices and Dean Ribble allotted $1000 to include copying, framing and incidentals. In November, 1946, the Fauquier County Board of Supervisors authorized the work "provided that said portrait be not removed from the wall."

As completion neared, faculty hopes for blackboards clashed with the artist's sensibilities. Mr. Silvette wrote the Dean "if the professors must have a blackboard, can't you get those moveable ones on stands —something like a painter's easel? At least it would then be a part of the furniture—not the decorative scheme." Mr. Campbell intervened to meet the demands of both aesthetes and professors. On November 12, 1947 John Marshall was hung well above the blackboards.

Figure 104 is a good copy of Washington's original despite the problems Silvette confronted by not being able to remove the original from the courthouse wall, where it hung high above the bench. It is also, like its original, an acceptable adaptation of Inman's great likeness of the chief justice.

Chapter 18

William James Hubard
(1807–1862)

I N HIS EARLY YOUTH Hubard, an expert in taking silhouettes, was known as "Master Hubard," a title that could be
fairly attributed to both his youth and his skill. He was
brought to this country from England in 1824 and continued his
art for another three or four years. But he came under the spell
of Stuart and others and soon gave up cutting for painting. Among
the last silhouettes he cut were a charming pair of John Quincy
Adams and his wife, sitting in their chairs, writing and reading,
taken just before the Adamses left the White House.[1] Within a
year or so Hubard had exhibited his paintings in Boston and
Philadelphia. In 1831 he moved to Baltimore and by 1838 was
established in Richmond. It was during this period he painted
his well-known series of diminutive full-length portraits of Marshall, Clay, Calhoun, Webster, Jackson, and Charles Carroll, one
or more of which can be seen in the University of Virginia, the
Corcoran Gallery of Art, the Metropolitan Museum of Art, and
elsewhere.

The course of Marshall's iconography with Hubard, as with so
many other artists, was a multiplication of the same likeness for
the chief justice and his sons and for others. Records of nine portraits of Marshall by or after Hubard can be found, and seven
portraits have been located. Of the known portraits, three are
bust-length and five others are small full-length seated figures,
but the facial likenesses all stem from the same source. All are full
face, all bear the same expression and the same treatment of Marshall's hair, and all show the same neckcloth or tie with almost
identical folds and long pointed ends. The full-length portraits
are smaller than those of bust size, and it can be conjectured that
the original was the full-length and the larger bust-size portraits
were later variations.

The exact date of the original Hubard life portrait is not known,
nor can we be sure which is the original. In the John Marshall
House in Richmond there is a typical small seated Marshall,

1. Oliver, *Portraits of John Quincy Adams,* 144.

painted by Hubard (fig. 105). It was a gift to the Association for the Preservation of Virginia Antiquities, in October 1959, from Mrs. Saunders Hobson. Mrs. Hobson's ancestor Charles Macmudo had lived for many years in Richmond at the corner of Sixth and Marshall streets. Nothing more is known of this painting, but since the photograph for figure 105 was taken, the portrait has been restored. For purposes of comparison with other Hubard portraits of Marshall, note the ends of the tie, the position of the hands, the landscape view at Marshall's left, and the shadow appearing in the light space at his right.

A comparable example is now owned by the University of Virginia (fig. 106). Little is known of its origin or former ownership. But we can compare the likeness with figure 105. The two are closely alike in all details, and in figure 106 the shadowy figure at Marshall's right appears to be a female figure on a pedestal. At his left, in the distant part of the landscape, appears a pedimented building with four columns and a brook running through the foreground. The building is perhaps a reminder of the capitol in Richmond, where Marshall had presided over sessions of the United States Circuit Court for Virginia.

A third example now belongs to Mrs. Virgil Fryman of Washington, Kentucky. According to family tradition Marshall sent the portrait to his nephew Martin Pickett Marshall, who went to Kentucky as a young man. The little portrait has probably been in the family since its origin. Mrs. Fryman, Martin Pickett Marshall's great-granddaughter, is the sixth generation of the family to live in the house known as Federal Hall, built by Marshall's brother Captain Thomas Marshall in 1800.[2] This portrait corresponds closely to the other two.

In 1920 at the American Art Association in New York, the collection of paintings belonging to Frank Bulkely Smith of Worcester, Massachusetts, was sold on April 22 and 23. Lot 119 (fig. 107) went for $250 to W. J. Kain.[3] It was then acquired by Thomas B. Clarke, and subsequently, in 1930, by Preston Davie of Tuxedo Park, New York. It appears that Mr. Davie gave the portrait to Paul D. Cravath and that it was later owned by his daughter Mrs. William F. Gibbs. It is now owned by Victor Spark of New York. Except for minor variations in locks of hair or in the shapes of the ends of the tie, the picture closely resembles the

2. Mrs. Virgil Fryman to the author, June 7, 1972.
3. American Antiquarian Society to the author, May 15, 1973.

105. John Marshall. Oil by William James Hubard, *ca.* 1834

6. John Marshall. Oil by William James
Hubard, *ca.* 1834

107. John Marshall. Oil by William James
Hubard, *ca.* 1834

others of this type. On the back of the canvas is written in ink,
"John Marshall by Hubard." On a label fastened to the back is
written, "Painted by Hubard" and, in a different hand, "Chief
Justice John Marshall 1755–1835, Congress 1799, Secretary of
War, 1800, [Secretary of] State, 1800, Chief Justice, 1801–1835,
President of the American Colonization Society, Vice President of
the American Bible Society."

Still another of this type belonged to John Gregg Thomas of
Baltimore, who was descended from Marshall's sister Elizabeth
Colston. It was exhibited at the Hubard exhibition in Richmond
in 1948. At that time Mr. Thomas, a great-great-nephew of Marshall's, said that according to family tradition the portrait was a
copy but that a restorer had deemed it an original. It is quite
likely that the restorer and family were both correct, except in the
meaning they applied to the words "copy" and "original." The
picture, of course, may be *the* original, or it may be simply one
more replica by Hubard. It passed from Mr. Thomas to his
daughter Mrs. Carl Barthel and now belongs to the National Por-

trait Gallery. In its reproduction here (fig. 108) the figure at the left can be clearly seen, and at the right side of the painting, at about the level of Marshall's mouth, may be picked out the pedimented building mentioned above. The only conspicuous difference is in the folds of the curtain over the little statue, which here hang down, while in other versions they are drawn upwards to a narrow point.

In 1870 there belonged to eighteen-year-old John Marshall of Piedmont Station, Fauquier County, Virginia, a great-grandson of Marshall's, a bust-length portrait of the chief justice described as by "Hubert" and "larger than life" and "said to be the best likeness ever painted of the Chief Justice." The lad's guardian was his aunt, Mrs. Ann Jones, a granddaughter of Marshall's. Dr. Louis Marshall, one of the chief justice's brothers, had been president of Washington College in 1830. The college later became Wash-

108. John Marshall. Oil by William James Hubard, *ca.*
1834

ington and Lee, and in 1870 General Robert E. Lee was its president. Mrs. Jones carried on an exchange of letters with President Lee that concluded with an arrangement whereby, in exchange for the portrait, young John Marshall received two years' free tuition at the college—the portrait being valued for the purpose at $500. Years later in 1910 the same John Marshall, then middle-aged, tried to redeem the portrait but without success. On December 16, 1934, the law school building at Washington and Lee, in which the portrait hung, was burned, and the portrait was destroyed.[4] Judging by its descent, this portrait must have been one of the Hubard replicas painted for Marshall's sons. We are fortunate in knowing what the portrait looked like, for it was reproduced in the *Green Bag* in 1901.[5] The reproduction was made from a poor photograph, or perhaps the portrait was in poor condition, but it shows clearly enough a close resemblance to figures 105 and 106. No size was mentioned, and there is no way to determine from the illustration whether the picture was larger than life.

Two versions of the bust portrait do survive. One (fig. 109), believed to have been painted in 1834, was said to have been given by Marshall to, or painted at the request of, his second son, Jaquelin Ambler Marshall of Prospect Hill, Fauquier County. The portrait was given to the John Marshall House in 1929 by the chief justice's granddaughter Mrs. Harrison Robertson, whose husband in 1890 had written of the picture: "The portrait of J. Marshall was painted by Hubard at Richmond from Life. It was given by him to his son, Dr. Jacquelin Ambler Marshall of 'Prospect Hill,' Fauquier Co. It hung in the parlor at 'Prospect Hill' until 1868 when after the death of Jacquelin Marshall's widow, in the division of family relics, it fell to the lot of my wife, Eliza C., a daughter of Jacquelin Marshall. It was considered by the family to be the best likeness ever taken of the Chief Justice."[6] This is a familiar claim, but the likeness is a sympathetic representation of the old chief justice as he appeared not much longer than a year or two before his death.

Another of this type (fig. 110) belongs to the Virginia His-

4. Allen W. Moger, "John Marshall's Portrait Used to Educate His Great-grandson," *Virginia Magazine of History and Biography*, LXIII (1955), 275–279.
5. *The Green Bag: An Entertaining Magazine for Lawyers*, XIII (1901), 231.
6. Note in possession of the Association for the Preservation of Virginia Antiquities, Richmond, signed by Harrison Robertson in 1890.

109. John Marshall. Oil by William James Hubard, *ca.* 1834

110. John Marshall. Oil by William Jam[es] Hubard, *ca.* 1834

torical Society, not in as good condition when photographed but still a fine likeness. Nothing is known of its past history.

There is an obscure reference by Mrs. John Lloyd, Hubard's daughter, that in 1901 a portrait of the seated version was hanging in the old Court of Appeals room in Capitol Square at Richmond. Its whereabouts are now unknown.

The number of Hubard portraits of Marshall is a good indication that it was a likeness favored by the family.

Chapter 19

John Frazee

(1790–1852)

ON APRIL 3, 1834, Colonel Thomas Handasyd Perkins, "Merchant Prince" of Boston and a generous benefactor of the Boston Athenaeum, wrote to the sculptor John Frazee in New York:

Sir: The consent of the Chief Justice of the United States, has been obtained to sit to you for his Bust – His official duties will prevent him from receiving you until the 22nd of May, when the Court sits in the City of Richmond, where he resides and I request you to proceed to that place, as near to the time named as possible.

In two days you should reach Baltimore and two more would place you at Richmond by the Steam Boat, or three if you come by way of this City [Washington], so that, if you leave New York on 16th May you will be in Richmond on the day appointed.

Should your attempt be successful, of which I have no doubt, you will be doubtless be called upon for duplicates.

Please, on the receipt of this, to write to me at this place *under cover*, to Mr. Webster, who will open the letter if I am absent. – Upon reflection it will be best to write *directly to Mr. Webster* and who will communicate with me and Judge Marshall should it be necessary. Please respond promptly. You are to receive $500.00 for the Bust, and your expenses to travel until you return to New York to be paid.[1]

Colonel Perkins's letter was accompanied by a note from Webster: "I have great pleasure in transmitting this, and hope you will find it convenient to wait on the Chief Justice, with your accustomed punctuality, as he has many engagements in various relations of life." [2] Frazee was not unknown to the Athenaeum. By now he had received commissions for five busts to be executed in marble for the Athenaeum at $500 each – Perkins, Story, John Lowell, Webster, and Nathaniel Bowditch – and he had the latter two almost completed. Hence Webster knew of his punctuality.

Frazee was one of America's pioneer sculptors working in plaster and marble. From a large family that was raised by his

---

1. Quoted in Mabel Munson Swan, *The Athenaeum Gallery, 1827–1873* (Boston, 1940), 145–146.
2. Daniel Webster to Frazee, *ibid.*, 147.

mother following his father's desertion, Frazee at age fourteen was apprenticed to a mason. The change from bricklaying to sculpture seemed a natural one, and before long he and his brother were engaged in cutting marble gravestones. Examples of his early work are in Trinity Church, New York City, and its chapel, St. Paul's. In 1824 he modeled Lafayette for the American Academy and was then elected to its membership. In 1831 he executed a handsome marble bust of John Jay for the Congress, for which he received $400. With a well-established reputation, he was a natural choice for the Athenaeum, which ultimately commissioned seven busts—the five mentioned above, William H. Prescott, and Marshall. In Frazee's later years his studio continued to turn out copies in plaster or marble of many of his more prominent busts.

In his autobiography Frazee wrote that upon receipt of Colonel Perkins's letter: "I started immediately for old Virginia and reached Richmond on the 21st day of May. I found Judge Marshall at his residence, and met with a frank and friendly reception from him. The next day he commenced sitting for his bust. On the 26th it was finished, packed up and put on board the packet for New York and I packed in the stage for home." [3] William Dunlap, the artist and diarist, records Frazee's passage back and forth through New York: "Friday 16th May 1834. Frazee (John) calls on me says he has written part of the memorandum for [me], is going to Richmond, Va. to take a bust of Judge [John] Marshall & will give me his memoir when he comes back. . . . Wedy [July] 23d. Frazee calls with a carriage & takes me to see his heads of Danl Webster & [Nathaniel] Bowditch. He has done well. Bowditch makes an ancient philosopher." [4] He also commented on Frazee: "He has progressed to a perfection which leaves him without a rival at present in the country. . . . At present Mr. Frazee is full of employment. . . . I have seen with admiration his bust of Daniel Webster, and with more than that of Dr. Bowditch: both chiseled in marble with skill and taste." [5] Marshall's own opinion of the bust is expressed in a testimonial he gave Frazee in May 1834, in which he wrote: "So far as I can rely on my

3. Quoted in *American Collector*, XV (1946), 12.
4. Dorothy C. Barck, ed., *Diary of William Dunlap, 1766–1839* . . . (New York, 1930), III, 787, 806.
5. William Dunlap, *History of the Rise and Progress of the Arts of Design in the United States* (Boston, 1834), II, 269.

own opinion [it] is admirably well executed. Others think it good too." [6]

What actually took place in Richmond between Marshall and Frazee is well told in a letter the sculptor wrote to the *New York Commercial Advertiser* on May 21, 1834:

I am here, sir, in old Virginia. I have had a very good time of it in coming on. No difficulties, no accidents, no breaking down, nor bursting of steam-boilers. All went along smoothly, by steam on land, and by steam on water. Nothing like steam, sir. . . . I like Richmond very well. It is up and down, straight along, and every way, just as nature formed it. . . . I hate your New York levelling system; there is no sense in it. The New Yorkers think they must bring everything in subservience to the passage of a carman's cart, laden with *rum and molasses*. . . . But in Richmond they can speak of hills and dales— and the city is much more picturesque and beautiful on account of those undulations. I have taken lodging on the hill, near the Capitol, a noble structure of Ionic Architecture, and near this is the City Hall, of the Doric order, both of which surpass in style and grandeur any public building we have in New York.

I must tell you something concerning my progress with the bust of Judge Marshall. I have taken two sittings; one more and I have him immortal. The venerable Chief Justice received me with every expression of kindness. His health is good, and he looks extremely well for one so advanced in years. He is drawing nigh to eighty. Yesterday he made me come and dine with him. He has no family about him excepting his domestics.—His wife, he tells me, was taken to a better world two years ago. While at dinner I asked him if he did not feel lone and melancholy since he was left companionless?—"Ah, yes," said the good and venerable sage, as the tears welled on his quivering eyelids;—"yes," he continued, "I do indeed feel the absence of a companion, so kind and good, and with whom I had lived with so much of harmony, love, and happiness, for more than forty years." "But," he added, "I submit with meekness and humility to the just will of Him, at whose appointed time we must all depart hence, and though he called her away, he has afforded me such health and strength, both body and mind, as have enabled me to bear up under the trying affliction."—He then went on to state that it seemed to be the constitution of his mind and nature to be cheerful in almost any condition of life. And indeed, I believe it, for I never met with a person of sweeter disposition, or a more even temperament.

When first consulting with him, as to how he would like to sit—He replied, "Just as *you* please, sir, suit your own convenience." I wanted

6. Quoted in Wayne Craven, *Sculpture in America* (New York, 1948), 88.

him to have an easy chair to sit in. "No," said he, "Don't trouble your-self for that, I can sit on any thing; I have been accustomed to every thing, in every stage of life; I have been in the army of the Revolution, and am used to sitting on logs and stones, and lying on the ground; *I am not particular.*" I asked if he could bear the fatigue of sitting more than an hour each time? "O, yes," he said, "I will sit for you as many hours, two, three or five, as you wish."

He has a firm constitution, and eats with a hearty appetite. When the cloth is removed, he takes two or three glasses of old Madeira Wine. He gave me some that he told me was thirty years old.

So you see that cheerfulness and vivacity contribute to longevity. Franklin was so,—Jefferson was so, and so was the elder Adams;—and all lived to a good old age;—and Judge Marshall seems likely to live to be as old as any one of them.[7]

Frazee made short work of his commission, and on May 26, Marshall signed a certificate reading: "This may certify that my bust made by Mr. Frazee so far as I can rely on my own opinion, is admirably well executed. Several of my friends in whose tastes and judgment I have great confidence have looked at it and pro-nounce it an excellent likeness."[8]

On June 19, 1834, the Athenaeum paid the sculptor's expenses of $102.[9] There was a little delay in making the final payment. Thomas W. Ward, treasurer of the Athenaeum, noted in his records in June 1834: "I have not directed any payment of the $200 asked for by Mr. Frazee thinking it would be time enough after he shall have sent the busts of Dr. Bowditch and Mr. Web-ster which were to have been delivered *here* 1st May."

Dunlap had one more note of Frazee's progress: "Thursday Octr 9th 1834. Receive a note from Frazee who has now 7 Busts to do for the Boston Athenaeum."[10]

Time was required, of course, to reproduce the plaster model in marble, but at last on August 8, 1835, Frazee was able to write, modestly, to Seth Bass, librarian of the Athenaeum:

I have just shipped to your Care the Busts of Judge Marshall and Col. Perkins. . . .

Now do, my dear Doctor, have great care of these Busts. They are works which I prize highly. You have none equal to them in your Athenaeum (in the modern sculptures) at least, such is my opinion,

7. *New York Commercial Advertiser,* June 5, 1834, 2.
8. Collection of Mrs. Margaret Frazee Belknap Heath, Tarrytown, N.Y.
9. Treasurer's Report, Jan. 5, 1835, Archives, Boston Athenaeum.
10. Barck, ed., *Diary of Dunlap,* III, 827.

and if your Boston Connoisseurs differ with me in this point please let me know the wherefore.

Take care how you unpack them, least [sic] you injure the marble; and I wish you to keep the muslin cloth round them until you have them in the place where you intend to exhibit them.—They never, in no case, should be handled without there being a cloth over them, to keep the hand from soiling the marble.[11]

The marble bust (fig. 111) now stands on the second floor of the Athenaeum. On the shoulder in back is cut the inscription, "John Marshall / by Frazee 1834," and on the small rectangular space at the top of the plinth in front is incised, "Presented / to the Boston Athenaeum / by Thos. H. Perkins." It is an undoubted, strong likeness and of such quality as not to deserve the comment of the lesser and later sculptor Loredo Taft that it was "a curiously rigid bust of John Marshall which with all its drapery offers a naked bosom to the executioner, as well as an old, wrinkled neck into which the small head seems to be withdrawn turtle-fashion."[12]

Colonel Perkins, who could pick up the scent of profit from a great distance, was not wrong when he had suggested to Frazee (probably as bait) that he would "doubtless be called upon for duplicates." His price was $60 for the single cast, $100 for six, and $150 for ten. Marshall himself placed an order with Frazee in February 1835: "I transmit you a check on the office of discount and deposit of the bank of the U.S. in Richmond for seventy dollars which you will I presume find no difficulty in using in New York. I am told your price for the casts of my bust is ten dollars. I am desirous of procuring seven of them. Have the goodness to present one of them to Mrs. Ledyard of New York and one to Mr. Justice Story of the Supreme Court. The other five I will thank you to forward to me by some vessel coming from New York to Richmond."[13]

Judge Story's copy was, at his death in 1845, bequeathed to Harvard College, with one of himself. In 1901 when Professor Thayer was preparing his centennial memorial of Marshall's becoming chief justice, the bust given to Harvard by Story seems to have been mislaid. Among the Thayer Papers at the Harvard Law School is a letter to Thayer from T. Tileston Baldwin dated April 11, 1901, in which Baldwin wrote: "There is no mention of this

11. Swan, *Athenaeum Gallery*, 146.   12. Quoted *ibid.*, 147.
13. Collection of Mrs. Heath.

111. John Marshall. Marble bust by John Frazee, 1834

112. John Marshall. Plaster bust by John Frazee, after 1834

bust in the University's list of portraits and busts; and Professor Ames and Mr. Arnold, at the Law School, and Mr. Kiernan, in the Library, of whom I made inquiries recently, have no knowledge of it." In my own search for Story's bequest I met with the same doubt, yet after a little exploration I found two plaster copies of the Athenaeum marble, true copies (almost Chinese copies), each still containing the inscription that it was presented to the Athenaeum by Thomas H. Perkins. One, pointed out to me by the late Professor Arthur E. Sutherland, is now placed high on the wall at an entrance to the Ames Court Room in Austin Hall, and the other, in poor condition and disfigured by some modern-day vandal, is in the great reading room of Langdell Hall, though which came from Judge Story is no longer known. Neither is it known to whom Marshall gave the others he bought.

A replica of the Athenaeum bust, in marble, stands beside the bench in the old historic Westmoreland County Courthouse in Montross, Virginia, bearing on the back of the shoulder "John Marshall by Frazee." Another marble is in the old Hall of Delegates room in the Virginia State Capitol Building in Richmond; inscribed on the front of the plinth is "Chief Justice Marshall" and on the shoulder in back, "J Fraxee Sculpt / 1850." Still another is in the Board of Estimate Chamber in New York's City Hall, not far from Frazee's marble of John Jay, but no record of its acquisition seems to have survived.

Some criticism was voiced about Marshall's bare breast and "exposed pectoral muscle," with the result that on at least one reproduction, that now owned by the New-York Historical Society by gift of A. S. Cozzens in 1953, the toga was raised to eliminate the exposure (fig. 112). It is in plaster and bears the simple inscription "John Marshall" on the back. There are undoubtedly many more of both varieties. In 1899 the Athenaeum entertained a proposal to have a gelatine mold taken of its marble original by one Caproni, but the outcome of the proposal is hidden.

The value and significance of Frazee's bust is that it is one of the last likenesses taken of the chief justice, only a year before he died, and yet it compares remarkably in likeness and character to the familiar portrait by Inman (fig. 73).

Chapter 20

Miscellaneous and
Posthumous Likenesses

A FEW PORTRAITS remain to be mentioned, some believed to have existed but now lost, some about which little is known, some in public places labeled "Marshall" but of doubtful attribution, and some that are posthumous likenesses. Mention of a few of these may lead to the discovery of lost portraits or to information concerning others.

James W. Ford (fl. 1833–1857)

In the Richmond *Whig* for June 18, 1835, a notice appeared that James W. Ford's portrait of Chief Justice Marshall, executed from life a few months previous to the death of the judge, "is now at his painting rooms, opposite the Eagle Hotel." Ford was a well-known painter; he was present at the Virginia Convention in 1829 and again in 1850 and advertised his profession from the 1830s to 1857. Among his friends was the artist John Blennerhassett Martin, who, it is said, tried in vain to convert him to Presbyterianism. Though many of his portraits are known, including several of Indian chiefs, his portrait of Marshall has not been found.

Horatio Greenough (1805–1852)

There is no doubt that Greenough worked on a bust of Marshall at least in the preliminary stages, though no evidence of the finished work has ever come to light. On February 21, 1828, Greenough wrote to his brother Henry, "I shall model Chief-Justice Marshall if he will sit." [1] A week later he wrote again, "I had this morning the first sitting from Chief-Justice Marshall. Judge Story says that any one would recognize my sketch; that

---

1. Frances Boott Greenough, ed., *Letters of Horatio Greenough to His Brother, Henry Greenough* . . . (Boston, 1887), 28.

it is capital." [2] A few days later John Quincy Adams, who was at the time sitting to Chester Harding for his portrait, wrote in his diary: "Walk to Mr. Harding's lodgings where I gave him a third sitting of about an hour for my portrait. Mr. Greenough was there waiting for Chief Justice Marshall whose bust he is taking." [3] Many years later Greenough's youngest brother, Richard (born in 1819), himself a sculptor, wrote from Rome to Frank Booth: "It is possible that Horatio may have modelled a bust of C. J. Marshall but I do not recall any such work. In any case, if he did, it is highly improbable that any cast of it is in existence." [4]

This is all we know, and we can only regret that we cannot see the chief justice as Greenough saw him in 1828.

Jane Value (1814–1891)

Jane Value was born in Hartford, Connecticut, and moved south in 1829 because of her mother's poor health, spending winters at Richmond, Charleston, and Columbia. She returned north in 1842 and married Dr. Joshua B. Chapin of Providence, Rhode Island, where she lived and died, leaving two daughters and a son. It is said that while in the South, "Miss Value is known to have painted at least one portrait from life, that of Chief Justice John Marshall." [5] She could not have been more than twenty-one years old at the time, and the portrait is lost.

Unknown

In the fall of 1969 Mrs. Mark Mitchell of Cincinnati presented to the Virginia Historical Society a portrait believed to be of Marshall (fig. 113). The artist is unknown, and the picture has an unknown provenance. It bears a faint if recognizable likeness to the chief justice but hardly can be said to be a satisfactory representation. Its nearest resemblance to other portraits of Marshall is

2. *Ibid.*, 31.

3. Diary of John Quincy Adams, Mar. 12, 1828, Adams Papers, Massachusetts Historical Society, Boston.

4. Mar. 13, 1901, Thayer Papers, Harvard University Law School, Cambridge, Mass.

5. Frederic Fairchild Sherman, "Newly Discovered American Miniaturists," *Antiques*, VIII (1925), 97.

113. John Marshall. Oil by an unknown artist

to that by Edward F. Peticolas (fig. 25), of which it might be a poor copy. And there is, of course, the possibility it may be one of the known portraits hitherto thought lost.

Hiram Powers (1805–1873)

The first posthumous likeness of Marshall was probably the bust commissioned shortly after Marshall's death for the old Superior Court Chamber on the second floor of the Capitol in Washington. Hiram Powers was selected for the work, and his marble (fig. 114) was completed in 1836 and took its place among those of the former chief justices. Powers was an able sculptor, but posthumous representations are rarely acceptable and this is no ex-

114. John Marshall. Marble bust by Hiram Powers, 1836

ception. It nevertheless occupies a distinguished spot in the
Capitol and is reproduced in *Compilation of Works of Art and
Other Objects in the United States Capitol* (Washington, D.C.,
1965), 186.

Randolph Rogers (1825–1892)

When the great Washington Monument in Richmond was being
planned, the sculptor Thomas Crawford was chosen for the project, which was designed on a magnificent scale. He completed
the monumental equestrian Washington and the figures of Jefferson and Patrick Henry, but he died in 1857 with much of the
work still to be done. The completion of the monument was given
to Randolph Rogers, who modeled the six allegorical figures and
the statues of Marshall, George Mason, Thomas Nelson, and General Andrew Lewis. Adeline Adams in her sketch of Crawford for
the *Dictionary of American Biography* describes the equestrian
Washington as "precariously set above a six-nosed plinth bearing
statues of six great Virginians" and characterizes the whole as a
work of "ingenuity rather than imagination."

When the statue of Marshall (fig. 115) was raised in 1869,
Richmond was still under military command. This prompted
Innes Randolph to pen the following verses:

> We are glad to see you, John Marshall, my boy,
>   So fresh from the chisel of Rodgers;
> Go take your stand on the monument there,
>   Along with the other old codgers;
> With Washington, Jefferson, Henry, and such,
>   Who sinned with a great transgression
> In their old-fashioned notions of freedom and right
>   And their hatred of wrong and oppression.
> You come rather late to your pedestal, John,
>   And sooner you ought to have been here,
> For the volume you hold is no longer the law,
>   And this—is no longer Virginia.
> The old Marshall law you expounded of yore
>   Is now not at all to the purpose,
> And the Martial Law of the new Brigadier
>   Is stronger than habeas corpus.
> So keep you the volume shut with care
>   For the days of the law are over;
> And it needs all your *brass* to be holding it there

115. John Marshall. Bronze statue by Randolph Rogers, after 1860

With "Justice" inscribed on the cover.
Could life awaken the limb of bronze
    And blaze in the burnished eye,
What would you do with your moment of life?
    Ye men of the days gone by!
Would ye chide us or pity us? blush or weep?
    Ye men of the days gone by!
Would Jefferson roll up the scroll he holds
    Which time has proven a lie?
Would Marshall close the volume of law
    And lay it down with a sigh? [6]

The likeness of Marshall stems from the Inman portrait and is perhaps as good as could be expected for such a monument. The whole structure with its seven large figures is quite impressive and suitable for the approach to Virginia's great capitol building.

Marshall as a Mason

There are two representations of Marshall as a Freemason. The earliest (fig. 116) is a stipple engraving done by J. A. O'Neill in 1874. Inscribed "Grand Master of Grand Lodge of Virginia Oct. 1793/ Engd. by J A O Neill, Hoboken, N.J.," it appeared in the *Proceedings of the M. W. Grand Lodge of Ancient York Masons of the State of Virginia.*[7] Though it is not known what portrait O'Neill followed, it may be that he had access to one of Harding's portraits and then tried to subtract thirty years in his copy.

The other Masonic likeness (fig. 117) was painted by David Silvette in 1954 for the Virginia Grand Lodge one year before the two hundredth anniversary of Marshall's birth. In 1793 Marshall had served as grand master of the Virginia Freemason's Lodge for two years. The likeness was unquestionably taken from the small French miniature (fig. 1) made in 1797 and therefore shows Marshall at approximately the age he was when grand master. The Masonic regalia visible in the portrait follows closely that in the O'Neill engraving. The portrait now hangs in the Masonic Temple in Richmond.

6. Marshall Papers, Swem Library, College of William and Mary, Williamsburg, Va.

7. James A. Goode, *Proceedings of the M. W. Grand Lodge of Ancient York Masons of the State of Virginia, from Its Organization in 1778 to 1822 . . .* (Richmond, 1874), I, following p. 120.

116. John Marshall. Engraving by J. A.
O'Neill, 1874

Hugh Cannon (1814–after 1857)

A well-executed posthumous bust of the chief justice (fig. 118) was made about 1840 by the sculptor Hugh Cannon, then living in Philadelphia. The bust was included in the Artist's Fund Society exhibition in 1840 and listed as the property of a "Peter McCall." It stands 27½ inches high, and a metal plaque fastened to the plinth is inscribed, "John Marshall / The Law Association of Philadelphia." The bust is now in the rooms of the Bar Association of Philadelphia, but its early history is unknown.

Bryant Baker (1881–   )

The county commission of Fauquier County, Virginia, employed the sculptor Bryant Baker of New York to make a statue of Chief Justice Marshall in 1959. The statue of the county's most famous son (fig. 119), unveiled in May 1959, was commissioned in observance of the Fauquier County Bicentennial. The likeness was

117. John Marshall. Oil by David Silvette, 1954

118. John Marshall. Marble bust by Hugh Cannon, 1840

said to have been taken from the then so-called Houdon head but made to appear older at the suggestion of the committee to procure the statue. Marshall appears dressed in a robe designed to conform to his own, which is preserved in Richmond in the John Marshall House. Cast in bronze in Astoria, Long Island, and set on a pedestal of polished granite, the statue is about six feet tall.

Seals and Medals

The first seal of Marshall College, Lancaster, Pennsylvania (fig. 120), adopted in 1836, is reproduced in Joseph Henry Dubbs's *History of Franklin and Marshall College* (Lancaster, Pa., 1903), 171. The likeness is said to have been taken from a portrait that a member of Marshall's family presented to the college. The por-

119. John Marshall. Bronze statue by Bryant Baker, 1959

120. John Marshall. Engraving of
the first seal of Marshall College

121. John Marshall and Benjamin
Franklin. Engraving of the first
seal of Franklin and Marshall
College

122. John Marshall and Benjamin
Franklin. Recent seal of Franklin
and Marshall College

123. John Marshall and George
Wythe. Bronze medallion by
Carl A. Roseberg, 1962

trait was probably one of the small Saint-Mémin engravings (fig. 13). A later seal (fig. 121), adopted when the institution was renamed Franklin and Marshall College, is also reproduced in Dubbs's volume. Still another (fig. 122) is the one in present use. The artists responsible for all of these are unknown, and the likenesses, at least in these reproductions of them, are remote.

For the Marshall-Wythe School of Law a bronze medal was designed in 1962 by the sculptor Carl A. Roseberg (fig. 123), 2¾ inches in diameter. The likeness of Marshall stems from a combination of the Saint-Mémin profile and the so-called Houdon head. It is a pity that it bears so little resemblance to the chief justice.

Modern Busts

In the possession of the College of William and Mary is a marble bust of Marshall (as well as busts of Sir William Blackstone and George Wythe) modeled by Felix G. W. de Weldon. It appears that when acquired by the William and Mary Law Association and placed on loan to the college, there was some question as to their artistic merit, and they have never been accepted by the State Fine Arts Commission. One can form his own opinion of their artistic merit from seeing the bust of Marshall, but in no particular whatever does it resemble its subject. It is a classic example of the risk of commissioning posthumous "likenesses."

Marshall University at Huntington, West Virginia, once owned a marble bust of Marshall executed by the sculptor Richard Flesch of Washington, D.C., which was destroyed by vandals in 1957. It was succeeded by a more lasting bronze bust designed and made by Professor Joseph Jublonski, a member of the faculty of the university, but it bears only a faint resemblance to the man.

There are, of course, other busts and portraits said to represent Marshall, but they do not stand the test. The Frick Art Reference Library has a photograph of a portrait said to be of Marshall and painted by William Dunlap, the art historian and diarist. The portrait can be traced back to the Ehrich Galleries, but any possible likeness to Marshall is missing.

Franklin and Marshall College possesses a marble bust that was sold as a bust of Marshall at the Erskine Hewitt sale by Parke Bernet in 1938. The sale price was $70, and the item was described in the catalog: "Guiseppi Ceracchi, American (Italian): 1751–1802 1131, John Marshall (Marble Bust) Portrait in the Roman style, the head slightly inclined to the left, beautifully draped in a toga; on round marble socle, with columnar marble pedestal. Total height of bust, 28 in., of pedestal 41 in. Collection of Mrs. Van Schaick, Albany, N.Y. and New York. From George D. Smith, New York." The difficulty with this bust is twofold. It simply does not in any respect resemble Marshall, and to have been modeled by Ceracchi it would have had to be done between 1791 and 1794, during part of which time Ceracchi was in America. At that time he did model busts of several prominent Americans—Washington, Jefferson, Adams, Hamilton, and Madison among others—but all for the purpose of furthering his own desire to be employed to execute a heroic "Monument Designed to Perpetuate the Memory of American Liberty." In those years Marshall would have been of no use to him in furthering this scheme, and indeed there is no record of Ceracchi ever having modeled such a bust. Almost at the time Marshall secured his fame by being chosen chief justice of the United States, Ceracchi lost his head in Paris by the guillotine, on January 31, 1801.

The list of false attributions continues, but it would serve little purpose to elaborate on them. The documented and proven portraits of the chief justice are many and fully sufficient to bring him back to our minds' eyes as he appeared during the third of a century he served as the great leader of the Supreme Court.

Index

Index

In this Index, John Marshall is designated as JM.

Adams, Adeline: on Washington Monument in Richmond, 183

Adams, George Washington (son of John Quincy Adams): views Harding's JM, 66

Adams, John, 2, 5, 6, 40, 71; likeness of, in Morse's *Old House of Representatives*, 41; bust of, by Ceracchi, 192

Adams, John Quincy, 2, 5, 42, 67, 111; portrait of, by Harding, 64; portrait of, by Healy, 147; silhouette of, by Hubard, 164; comments on Greenough's bust of JM, 180

Adams, Samuel, 158

Agassiz, Elizabeth C.: on Harding as an artist, 64

Allan, Mrs. Louisa G., 108

Allston, Washington: as roommate of S. F. B. Morse, 40

Amartico, Joseph, 149

Ambler, Cary: visits JM before his operation, 136

Ambler, Jaquelin (father-in-law of JM), 6

Ambler, Mary Willis. *See* Marshall, Mrs. John

American Art Association, 165

American Bank Note Company: use of Inman likeness of JM by, 146

American Colonization Society, 142, 167

American Eloquence: Jackman's engraving in, 156; illustrated, 157

American Magazine of Useful and Enlivening Knowledge: engraving of JM in, 155

American Orator's Own Book, The: Welch's engraving in, 156; illustrated, 157

American Scenic and Historic Preservation Society, Philipse Manor, Yonkers, N.Y.: owner of Chambers's JM, 144

Analectic Magazine and Naval Chronicle: reproduction of Wood's engraving of JM in, 35

Andrews, Eliphalet F.: copy of Inman's JM by, 154, illustrated, 153

Archer, Lizzie, 45

Arnason, H. Harvard: on Houdon, 16, 17n

Arnold, John H. (librarian of Harvard Law School), 155

Association for the Preservation of Virginia Antiquities: given custody of John Marshall House, 22–23. *See also* John Marshall House

Association of the Bar of the City of New York, 48, 50, 156; Thompson likeness of JM at, 31, illustrated, 32; wax bust of JM by Hughes at, 96, 97, 98, 99

Attler, W. S., 108

Austin Hall, Harvard Law School: bust of JM by Frazee at, 178

Avery, Samuel P., 13

Bainbridge, Commo. William: portrait of, by Jarvis, 54

Baker, Bryant: statue of JM by, 186, illustrated, 189

Baldwin, Christopher, 74

Baldwin, T. Tileston, 175

Baltimore, Md. *See* Johns Hopkins University; Walters Art Gallery

Bar Association. *See* Association of the Bar of the City of New York; Philadelphia Bar Association

Bar Library Company of Baltimore: Wattles's portrait of JM at, 85, 87, illustrated, 86

Barlow, Joel: bust of, by Houdon, 9, 15

Barthel, Mrs. Carl, 167

Bass, Seth (librarian of the Boston Athenaeum), 174

Baxter, Mrs. Norman, 58

Bayley, Frank W., 33

Beveridge, Albert J.: Jarvis JM in *Life of John Marshall* by, 61

Binney, Horace, 60

Binney, Mrs. M. L., 28

Black, Mrs. Alexander Leslie, 67

Black Hawk (Indian chief), 104

Blackstone, William, 191

Blakeman, Thomas: etching of JM after Inman by, 156, illustrated, 157

Blérancourt, Chateau de. *See* Musée de la Coopération Franco-Américaine

Boilly, Louis: painting of Houdon's studio by, 16

Bolton, Mrs. Ethel S.: describes wax bust of JM by Hughes, 98

Boone, Daniel, 64

Boston Athenaeum, 67, 125; Harding's portrait of JM commissioned by, 72–73, illustrated, 75; Frazee's bust of JM commissioned for, 171, illustrated, 176; other busts commissioned by, 171

Boston Evening Transcript: evaluation of Harding as an artist in, 64

Bowditch, Nathaniel: statue of, by Hughes, 97; bust of, by Frazee, 171–172

Bowdoin College Museum of Art: Thompson likeness of JM on loan to, 33, illustrated, 33

Bowen, Daniel, 151

Bower, R. M., 50

Boykin, Mrs. Ann, 31

Bradley, Justice Joseph P.: account of Saint-Mémin's JM by, 19, 23; on R. Peale's porthole portrait of JM, 50; procures Martin JM for U.S. Supreme Court, 87

Brandagee, Frank B., 146

Brockenbrough, Col. John, 55

Brook, The, New York City: owner of Eichholtz copy of Inman's JM, 143, illustrated, 143

Brooke, Richard Norris: copy of W. D. Washington's JM by, 161, 162, 163, illustrated, 161; portrait saved from fire by, 162

Brooklyn Museum, 40

Brooks, C. A., 50

Browere, John Henry Isaac, 2, 4, 118

Brown, Charles, 122

Brown, Gen. Jacob Jennings: portrait of, by Jarvis, 54

Brown, James, 31

Brown, John Herbert: owner of so-called Houdon bust, 9

Brown, Mrs. Margaret Dandridge Williams: owner of so-called Houdon bust, 9, 12

Brown, William Henry
portraits of JM by: as stamped on cover of his *Portrait Gallery*, 121, illustrated, 122; at Massachusetts Historical Society (2), 121, 122, 125, illustrated, 123, 124; as lithographed in *Portrait Gallery*, 125, illustrated, 126; at Virginia Historical Society, paired with W. C. Moore, 125, illustrated, 127; at Virginia Historical Society, 125–127, illustrated, 128

Bruce, Malcolm, 42

Bruton Parish Church, Williamsburg, Va.: proposal of, for Marshall window, 79, 80, 82

Bryan, St. George T. C., 120

Burr, Aaron, 2; trial of, 18, 19

Butler, Benjamin F.: Martineau comment on, 52
Byrnes, Joseph E., 85

Cadwalader, John L., 96
Calhoun, John C.: portrait of, by Hubard, 164
Campbell, Edmund S., 163
Cannon, Hugh: bust of JM by, 186, illustrated, 188
Capitol. *See* United States Capitol; Virginia State Capitol
Caproni, Mr.: and proposed mold of Frazee's bust of JM, 178
Carroll, Charles, of Carrollton: portrait of, by Harding, 66; portrait of, by Hubard, 164
Carroll, Gov. Charles, of Maryland, 96
Carter, Ledyard, and Milburn: owners of Jarvis JM (fig. 39), 62
Catlin, George, 4, 127; and his paintings of Indian chiefs, 52–53; at Virginia Constitutional Convention, 113; paints miniature of Dolley Madison, 115; paints Virginia Constitutional Convention, with key, 115, illustrated, 116, 117, 119
Century Association: and Jarvis portrait of JM in *Portraits Owned by Clubs of New York*, 58
Century Illustrated Monthly Magazine: engraving of Saint-Mémin's JM in, 21; Chappel's engraving of JM in, 91
Ceracchi, Guiseppe: bust purporting to be of JM by, 192
Chambers, William B.: copy of Eichholtz portrait of JM after Inman by, 144, illustrated, 143
Chapin, Dr. Joshua B., 180
Chappel, Alonzo: engraving of JM by, 85, 90–91, 92, illustrated, 91
Chase, Chief Justice Salmon P., 50, 144
Childs, Cephas G.: as Inman's partner, 138

Chrétien, Gilles-Louis: inventor of the physiognotrace, 18
Clarke, Thomas B. (collector): and Lambdin portrait of JM after Inman, 149; owner of Hubard JM, 165
Clay, Henry: Martineau comment on, 52; portrait of, by Healy, 147; portrait of, by Hubard, 164
Cochrane, Alexander S. (collector): former owner of Chambers's JM after Inman, 144
Cole, T. Willoughby, 111
Colston, Edward: former owner of so-called Houdon bust of JM, 10
Colston, Mrs. Rawleigh (Elizabeth Marshall, JM's sister), 167; former owner of so-called Houdon bust of JM, 10
Connecticut State Library: owner of Inman likeness of JM, 146, illustrated, 145
Converse, Sherman: former owner of Morse's *Old House of Representatives*, 41
Copley, John Singleton, 1, 4, 40
Copy: defined, ix
Corcoran, William Wilson, 23
Corcoran Gallery of Art, Washington, D.C., 18, 23, 164; owner of Morse's *Old House of Representatives*, 41; owner of R. M. Sully JM, 108
Cozzens, A. S., 178
Cranch, John: copy of Harding JM by, 71, illustrated, 71
Cravath, Paul D., 165
Craven, Wayne: on Hughes as sculptor, 98
Crawford, Thomas: designer of Washington Monument in Richmond, 183
Cronkhite, Elisha P., 79
Custis, Parke, 27

Daguerre, Louis Jacques Mandé, 1
Dana, Francis, 6
Danforth, Allen (comptroller of Harvard College), 77

Davie, Preston, 165
Davies, John W., 85
Davis, Isaac P.: procures frame for
    Harding JM, 73
Delaplaine, Joseph, 36, 37n
Dickson, Harold E.: on Jarvis's
    portraits of JM, 55; on J. M.
    Thayer's Jarvis portrait of JM,
    57
Dickson, Samuel, 23
Dillon, John F.: describes Sully
    JM (fig. 60) in his *John
    Marshall: Life, Character and
    Judicial Services,* 111
Doggett and Company, John. *See*
    John Doggett and Company
Domet, Jacques, 15
Donaldson, Thomas C.: former
    owner of Catlin's *Virginia Con-
    stitutional Convention,* 120
Draper, Lyman C. (secretary of the
    State Historical Society of Wis-
    consin), 104, 106, 108
Duke University, 156; owner of
    Saint-Mémin's drawing (fig.
    10), 19, illustrated, 20; be-
    quest to, from E. C. Marshall,
    23
Dunlap, William: Cranch's portrait
    of JM in *History of the Rise
    and Progress of the Arts* by,
    72; mentions Frazee in *Diary,*
    172; portrait of JM attributed
    to, 191
Durand, Asher Brown: engraving
    after Inman by, 138–139, il-
    lustrated, 142

Edmundson, J. S., 50
Edouart, Auguste: silhouette of JM
    by, 129, illustrated, 130
Edwin, David: engraving of JM by,
    28, 31, illustrated, 30
Eichholtz, Elizabeth (daughter of
    Jacob Eichholtz), 144
Eichholtz, Jacob: copies of Inman's
    JM by, 141–144, illustrated,
    142, 143
Eliot, Henry Ware, 71
Ellis, Thomas H., 108
Elmhurst, Mrs. Leonard K., 154

Elyria (steamer): brings W. W.
    Story's statue of JM to New
    York, 131
Emerson, Edward M.: describes
    JM, 76
Evans, James, 125

Fairmount Park, Philadelphia: site
    of statue of JM by W. W.
    Story, 133, illustrated, 132
Fauquier County, Virginia, Court-
    house: W. D. Washington's
    portrait of JM at, 158, 163, il-
    lustrated, 160
Feke, Robert, 1
Fisher, George D.: correspondence
    of, on JM portraits, 24, 139,
    141
Flesch, Richard: bust of JM by, 191
Folger, Charles I. (secretary of the
    Treasury), 132
Ford, James W.: portrait of JM by,
    179
Franklin, Benjamin, 9, 15, 16
Franklin and Marshall College:
    likeness of JM on seal of, 191,
    illustrated, 190; owner of so-
    called Ceracchi bust, 191–192
Frazee, John, 3, 4, 5; bust of JM
    commissioned from, by Boston
    Athenaeum, 171, illustrated,
    176; JM's meeting with, 173–
    174; sends bust to Athenaeum
    with instructions for handling,
    174–175; duplicates bust and
    sells 10 copies to JM, 175;
    modifies bust to meet criticism,
    178; modified bust at New-
    York Historical Society, illus-
    trated, 177
Frick Art Reference Library, 58,
    85, 191
Frothingham, James, 44
Fryman, Mrs. Virgil: owner of
    Hubard portrait of JM, 165
Fulton, Robert: bust of, by Hou-
    don, 9, 15

Garvan, Francis P., 28
Garvan, Mabel Brady, 28

Gatewood, Mrs. John M.: owner of Peticolas's JM, 31, illustrated, 32

Gerry, Elbridge, 6

Giacometti, Georges: on Houdon, 15

Gibbs, Mrs. William F., 165

Gilcrease, Thomas, Institute of American History and Art. *See* Thomas Gilcrease Institute of American History and Art

Giles, Gov. William R., 112

Gilman, Daniel Coit, 15

Goodwin, Rev. William A. R., 80

Graham, Robert B., Jr.: on portrait of JM by Silvette, 162

Grant, William, 67

Gray, Francis C.: as vice-president of Boston Athenaeum, commissions Harding portrait of JM, 72

Gray, Justice Horace, 59, 158; on Harding portrait of JM, 69

Green Bag, The: R. Peale JM in, 52; Harding JM in, 69, 79; Brown silhouette of JM in, 127; Hubard JM in, 169

Greenough, Henry, 179

Greenough, Horatio, 1; bust of JM by, 65, 179

Greenough, Richard: doubts of, as to existence of Horatio Greenough's JM, 180

Grigsby, Hugh Blair, 114

Gruppe, Karl H.: and his medallic likeness of JM, 26, 34, illustrated, 25

Gwathmey, Mrs. Francis, 85

Hall, Edward E., 74

Hall of Fame, New York University: Herbert Adams's bust of JM at, 16, illustrated, 17; and its Gruppe medal of JM, 26, 34, illustrated, 25

Hamilton, Alexander: statue of, by Hughes, 97; bust of, by Ceracchi, 192

Harding, Chester, 4, 5, 127; portraits of Supreme Court justices by, 65, 66; meeting of, with JM, 73; at quoit club with JM, 74; measures JM's head, 76; borrows Athenaeum portrait to paint replica, 77; account of Virginia Constitutional Convention by, 114; paints John Quincy Adams, 180

portraits of JM by: at Harvard, 65, 66, illustrated, 68; at Washington and Lee University, 67, illustrated, 69; at Tulane University, 69, 70, illustrated, 70; at Boston Athenaeum, 72–74, illustrated, 75

Hardy, Mrs. Sally Marshall, 24

Harris, C. X., 143

Harris-Ewing, of Washington, D.C. (photographers), 50

Harrison, Joseph, Jr.: Catlin's paintings pledged with, 118

Hart, Charles Henry: on W. H. Brown, 125

Hart, John (Richmond dealer), 120

Harvard Law School: receives legacy of Harding JM from Joseph Story, 67; acquires replica of Harding's Athenaeum JM, 77

Harvie, Ann F., 24, 85, 158; former owner of Inman's replica of JM, 141

Harvie, Emily, 158; former owner of Inman's replica of JM, 141

Harvie, Jacquelin B., 55

Hayden, Rev. Horace Edwin, 93

Hayward, Dr. George, 77

Healy, George Peter Alexander: copy of Inman's portrait of JM by, 147, illustrated, 148; other portraits by, 147

Henry, Patrick, 55

Herring, James: reproduces Durand engraving of JM in *National Portrait Gallery of Distinguished Americans,* 138–139, illustrated, 142

Higgins, Mrs. Kenneth R., 23, 146

Historical Society of Pennsylvania: Eichholtz copy of Inman's JM at, 141, illustrated, 143

Hobart, Rt. Rev. Henry, bishop of New York: bas-relief of, by Hughes, 97

Hobson, Mrs. Saunders, 165

Holmes, Justice Oliver Wendell: portrait of, in Langdell Hall, 77

Houdon, Jean Antoine, 6; as possible sculptor of bust of JM, 9, 15; other busts by, 9, 15, 16

House of Representatives. See *Old House of Representatives, The*

Howe, Mrs. Mark DeWolfe, 122

Hubard, William James, 3, 4, 5, 164, 169
portraits of JM by: at John Marshall House (2), 164–165, 169, illustrated, 166, 170; at University of Virginia, 165, illustrated, 167; owned by Victor Spark, 165, illustrated, 167; at National Portrait Gallery, 167–168, illustrated, 168; at Virginia Historical Society, 169–170, illustrated, 170

Hughes, Robert Ball, 3; wax bust of JM by, 96–99, illustrated, 97

Hull, Commo. Isaac: portrait of, by Jarvis, 54

Humphrey, Hon. James, 52

Huntington, Charles, 41

Huntington, Daniel, 41

Huntington, Rev. William A. R., 80

Independence National Historical Park, Independence Hall, Philadelphia: owner of Knapp's copy of Inman's JM, 152, illustrated, 153

Indians, American: C. B. King's portraits of, 53; Catlin's portraits of, 53, 118, 120

Inman, Henry, 3, 4, 127, 134; original portrait of JM by, 136, 138, illustrated, 135; partner of Cephas G. Childs, 138; replica portrait of JM by, 139, illustrated, 140; authorizes A. B. Durand to engrave replica, 139

Jackman, William G.: engraving of JM after Inman by, 156, illustrated, 157

Jackson, Andrew: portrait of, by Healy, 147; portrait of, by Hubard, 164

Jamestown Foundation: Inman's replica of JM on loan to, 141

Jarvis, John Wesley, 1, 3, 4; in partnership with Joseph Wood, 35; apprenticed to Edward Savage, 54; portraits by, in New York City Hall, 54
portraits of JM by: owned by R. C. Marshall, 55, illustrated, 56; owned by J. M. Thayer, 57–58, illustrated, 57; at Gilcrease Institute, 58–59, illustrated, 59; at White House, 59–61, illustrated, 60; owned by Carter, Ledyard, and Milburn, 62–63, illustrated, 63

Jay, John: bust of, by Frazee, 171, 178

Jefferson, Thomas, 2, 27, 48, 53, 192; appearance of, in old age, 5; bust of, by Houdon, 9, 15; likeness of, in Morse's *Old House of Representatives*, 41

John Doggett and Company: framer of Harding's Athenaeum JM, 74

John Marshall Hotel: portrait of JM at, 146, illustrated, 145; lucite key tag of, 146, illustrated, 147

John Marshall House, 25, 42
portraits in, by or after: Houdon (so-called) 9, 10, 16; Saint-Mémin, 22; Thompson, 31, 33; Thomas Marshall, 45; Jarvis, 62; Inman, 146; Hubard, 164, 169

Johns Hopkins University: owner of reproduction of so-called Houdon bust, 13, 15, illustrated, 14; owner of Thompson portrait of JM, 28, illustrated, 29

Johnston, John Taylor, 14

Jones, A. D.: Orr's engraving in his *Illustrated American Biography*, 155, illustrated, 156

Jones, Mrs. Ann, 168, 169

Jones, John Paul: bust of, by Houdon, 9, 15

Jublonski, Joseph: bust of JM by, 191

Kain, W. J., 165

Kearny, Francis: engraved portrait of JM by, 35, 37, illustrated, 36

Keats, John, 2

Kellogg, E. B. and E. C. (lithographers): Brown silhouette of JM lithographed by, 121, 125, illustrated, 126

Kemper, Charles: rescues W. D. Washington's portrait of JM, 158

Kemper, Theodore, 158

King, Charles Bird, 4, 44, 53

Kirby, Allen P.: donor of Peticolas's portrait of JM to Lafayette College, 42

Klackner, Christian: copy of Saint-Mémin's JM by, 21, 22, illustrated, 22

Knapp, George K.: copy of JM after Inman by, 152, illustrated, 153

Knoedler Galleries, 59

Lafayette, Marie Joseph Paul Yves Roch Gilbert du Motier, marquis de: bust of, by Houdon, 9, 15; on Houdon's Washington, 9; portrait of, by Morse, 40; Catlin sends sketches to, 118; bust of, by Frazee, 172

Lafayette College: Peticolas's portrait of JM at, 42, illustrated, 43

Lambdin, Emma C. (daughter of J. R. Lambdin): on her father's portrait of JM, 149, 151

Lambdin, George C.: portrait of JM after Inman by, 147, illustrated, 150

Lambdin, James Reid: portraits of JM after Inman by, 147, illustrated, 150

Landis, Benjamin F.: portrait of JM after Harding by, 79

Langdell Hall, Harvard Law School: Harding replica of JM at, 77; busts of JM by Frazee at, 178

Law Association of Philadelphia. *See* Philadelphia Bar Association

Lawrence, Charles B., 36

Ledyard, Lewis Cass, Jr., 62

Ledyard, Lewis Cass, III, 62

Lee, Gen. Robert E.: president of Washington and Lee College, 169

Lees, Mrs. S. P.: owner of missing portrait of JM, 85, 91

Lewis, Gen. Andrew: statue of, by Rogers, 183

Lewis, John Frederick (collector), 152

Lewis, Lunsford L., 83

Library of Congress, 48, 144, 156

Lile, William Minor, 83

Livingston, Justice Brockholst: likeness of, in Morse's *Old House of Representatives*, 41; former owner of Jarvis portrait of JM, 62, 63

Lloyd, Mrs. John (daughter of W. J. Hubard), 170

Longacre, James B.: reproduces Durand engraving of JM in *The National Portrait Gallery of Distinguished Americans*, 138–139, illustrated, 142

Long Island Historical Society: former owner of R. Peale's replica of JM, 52

Louis Philippe, king of France: commissions portrait of JM by Healy, 147, illustrated, 148

Lowell, John: bust of, by Frazee, 171

Lowndes, William, 38

Lucas, George A.: and his diary entries relating to so-called Houdon bust, 13, 14, 15

Ludwig, Dr. Allen: owner of bust of JM by Hughes, 98, 99

McCall, Peter, 186
Macdonough, Thomas: portrait of, by Jarvis, 54
McKean, Joseph, 76
Macmudo, Charles, 165
McNeil, Mrs. J. V., 149
Madison, Dolley: aids Catlin's wife, 115
Madison, James: at Virginia Constitutional Convention, 74, 113, 114, 115; bust of, by Ceracchi, 192
Marbury, William L.: owner of Martin portrait of JM, 87, 92, illustrated, 89
Marshall, Charles (brother of JM), 88
Marshall, Charles E. A.: owner of portrait of JM, 33, illustrated, 33; owner of portrait of "dearest Polly," 45, illustrated, 46
Marshall, Edward Carrington (youngest son of JM), 55; opinion of, on Inman portrait of JM, 141
Marshall, Edward Carrington (great-grandson of JM), 23
Marshall, Elizabeth. *See* Colston, Mrs. Rawleigh
Marshall, Mrs. Humphrey (Mary Marshall, sister of JM), 8
Marshall, Jaquelin Ambler (second son of JM), 169
Marshall, Jaquelin Ambler (grandson of JM), 55
Marshall, John, 2, 3, 4, 5; appearance and dress of, 5, 93, 98, 104, 122, 134, 173–174; and XYZ mission, 6; at Virginia ratifying convention of 1788, 6; marriage of, 6; on Houdon's statue of Washington, 9; and his *Life of Washington,* 9, 77; best likeness ever taken of, 10, 21, 60, 61, 134, 139, 169; sits to Saint-Mémin, 19; painted by Thompson, 28; sits to Wood,

36; sits to Morse, 38; painted by E. F. Peticolas, 42; sits to R. Peale, 48; comments on Peale's porthole portrait of Washington, 48; painted by Jarvis, 55; sits to Harding, 65, 66, 73; described by Harding, 73–74; head of, measured by Harding, 76; sits to Martin, 85; wax bas-relief of, by Waugh, 93; wax bust of, by Hughes, 96; comment of, on R. M. Sully, 100–101; painted by R. M. Sully, 101; painted by Catlin at Virginia Constitutional Convention, 112, 114; silhouettes of, by Brown, 121; portrait of, commissioned by Philadelphia Bar Association, 134; undergoes operation for the stone, 136–137; tribute of, to Dr. Physick, 137–138; as chairman of Virginia Colonization Society, 143; said to have sat to J. R. Lambdin, 149; painted by Hubard, 164; presides over U.S. Circuit Court for Virginia, 165; sits to Frazee, 173–174; comment of, on Frazee bust, 174; painted by Jane Value, 180; appearance of, as Freemason, 185. *For specific likenesses, see entries for individual artists and the list of Illustrations (pp. ix–xviii); see also* Medals; Miniatures; Seals; Portraits lost or unlocated
Marshall, John, Jr., 6
Marshall, John (great-grandson of JM): and the exchange of a Hubard portrait of JM for tuition, 168
Marshall, Mrs. John (Mary Willis Ambler): marriage of, 6; pastel of, 7, illustrated, 7 (see also frontispiece); locket miniature of, 8, illustrated, 8; portrait of, by Thomas Marshall, 45, illustrated, 46; correspondence of, with JM prior to his operation, 136; death of, 138

Marshall, John, Hotel. *See* John Marshall Hotel

Marshall, Dr. Louis (brother of JM): as president of Washington College, 168

Marshall, Margaret. *See* Smith, Mrs. Thomas Marshall

Marshall, Martin Pickett (nephew of JM), 165

Marshall, Mary (sister of JM). *See* Marshall, Mrs. Humphrey

Marshall, Mary (daughter of JM): Inman's replica of JM given to, 139, illustrated, 140

Marshall, Mary Willis Ambler. *See* Marshall, Mrs. John

Marshall, Rebecca Snowden: owner of bas-relief of JM by Waugh, 96, illustrated, 95

Marshall, Richard Coke (great-great-great-grandson of JM), 55

Marshall, Richard Stribling (great-grandson of JM), 55

Marshall, Mrs. Robert E. Lee, 96

Marshall, Capt. Thomas (brother of JM), 165

Marshall, Thomas (son of JM): and his portrait of his mother, 45, illustrated, 46

Marshall, Walton, 23

Marshall House. *See* John Marshall House

Marshall College: first seal of, 188. *See also* Franklin and Marshall College

Marshall University: and its bust of JM, 191

Marshall-Wythe School of Law, College of William and Mary: portrait of JM after Inman at, 152, illustrated, 153; and its medallion likeness of JM, 191, illustrated, 190

Martin, John Blennerhassett, 3, 4, 179

portraits of JM by: at University of Virginia, 83–84, illustrated, 84; at U.S. Supreme Court, 87, illustrated, 88; owned by William L. Marbury, 87–88, illustrated, 89; lost portrait, 90, illustrated, 91

Martineau, Harriet: on a scene in the Supreme Court, 52

Maryland Historical Society: and its portrait of JM by G. C. Lambdin, 149, 156, illustrated, 150

Mason, George: statue of, by Rogers, 183

Masonic Temple, Richmond: portrait of JM by Silvette at, 185, illustrated, 187

Massachusetts Historical Society: 33, 77; Brown's silhouettes of JM at, 122, illustrated, 123, 124

Maverick, Peter R., 36

Mayo, G. W., 108

Medals: likeness of JM on, 25, 26, 191

Meeker, Arthur, 33

Meigs, Montgomery C., 48

Mellon, Andrew, 149

Mercer, Dr. William Newton: and Washington and Lee's Harding portrait of JM, 67

Merchants Club, New York City: owner of Landis portrait of JM after Harding, 79

Merhige, Judge Robert R., Jr., of U.S. District Court: portrait of JM in chambers of, 146, illustrated, 145

Metropolitan Museum of Art, 164

Meyers, William Barksdale: portrait of JM after Inman by, 147, illustrated, 148

Michaelson, Cornelius, 90

Middleboro, Mass., 27

Middleton, Daniel Wesley (clerk of the U.S. Supreme Court): portrait of JM by, 60, 144, 146, illustrated, 145

Miniatures: of JM, 6 (see also frontispiece), 24; of Mrs. John Marshall, 8, 45

Mitchell, James T.: on Inman's portrait of JM, 134

Mitchell, Mrs. Mark, 180

Mitchill, Dr. Samuel Latham, 55

Molière (Jean Baptiste Poquelin): bust of, by Houdon, 16
Monroe, James: and Virginia Constitutional Convention, 74, 113, 114, 115
Montague, Mrs. Jeffrey G. A.: portrait of JM after Inman by, 146, illustrated, 148
Moore, Frank: Jackman's engraving in his *American Eloquence*, 156, illustrated, 157
Moore, Richard Channing: silhouette of, by Brown, 125, illustrated, 127
Morris, Robert, 158
Morse, Rev. Jedediah (father of S. F. B. Morse), 40
Morse, Nathan, 60
Morse, Samuel Finley Breese: *Old House of Representatives* by, 38, 40–41, 141, illustrated, 39
Musée de la Coopération Franco-Américaine, in Chateau de Blérancourt, Aisne, France: Healy portrait of JM at, 147, illustrated, 148

National Academy of Design: Morse a founder of, 40–41
National Gallery of Art, Washington, D.C., 77, 149
National Portrait Gallery, Washington, D.C.: J. R. Lambdin portrait of JM at, 149; Hubard portrait of JM at, 167–168
Nelson, Thomas: statue of, by Rogers, 183
Newhouse, Samuel I., 61
Newsam, Albert: lithograph of Inman's portrait of JM by, 138
New York City. *See* Brook, The; Merchants Club; New-York Historical Society; New York City Hall; Hall of Fame, New York University; Pierpont Morgan Library; University Club
New York City Hall, 40, 54; Frazee bust of JM at, 178
New-York Historical Society: Jarvis a member of, 54; Catlin drawings bought by, 118; Catlin's

Virginia Constitutional Convention and key acquired by, 120, illustrated, 116, 117; Frazee bust of JM at, 178, illustrated, 177
New York *Mirror*, 97
New York University. *See* Hall of Fame, New York University
Nickolas, C. (cashier of U.S. Bank), 55
Niles' Weekly Register, 137
Norton, Mrs., 62

Old House of Representatives, The: painting by Morse, 38, 40, 41, illustrated, 39, 40
Oneida (steamship): wrecked with Edouart aboard, 129
O'Neill, J. A.: engraving of JM as a Mason by, 185, illustrated, 186
Orr, John W.: engraving of JM after Inman by, 155, illustrated, 156
Outlook: Brown silhouette of JM in, 125, illustrated, 124

Paine, Thomas: engraving of, by Rogers, 158
Parke Bernet Gallery, 31, 90, 191
Paul, Jeremiah: portrait of JM attributed to, 28, 34
Payne, John Barton, 110–111
Peale, Charles Willson, 1, 4, 33, 48
Peale, Rembrandt, 28, 37, 48, 98 portraits of JM by: at U.S. Supreme Court, 48, 50, illustrated, 49; at Virginia Museum of Fine Arts, 50, 52, illustrated, 51
Pennsylvania Academy of the Fine Arts, 138; portrait of JM after Inman at, 152; illustrated, 153
Pennsylvania Museum of Art: owner of W. W. Story statue of JM, 133, illustrated, 132
Perkins, Thomas Handasyd: commissions bust of JM from Frazee, 171, illustrated, 176; correspondence of, with Frazee, 171, 175
Perry, Commo. Oliver Hazard: portrait of, by Jarvis, 54

Peticolas, Edward F., 42, 180–181; portrait of JM after Thompson by, 42, 44, illustrated, 43

Peticolas, Jane Braddock: portrait of JM after Thompson by, 31, illustrated, 32

Philadelphia. *See* Fairmount Park; Historical Society of Pennsylvania; Independence National Historical Park; Pennsylvania Academy of the Fine Arts; Pennsylvania Museum of Art; Philadelphia Bar Association; Union League of Philadelphia

Philadelphia Bar Association: copy of Saint-Mémin's JM at, 23; Inman's portrait of JM commissioned by, 134–136, illustrated, 135

Physick, Dr. Philip Syng, 134, 136, 137

Pickering, Timothy: portrait of, by Harding, 66

Pierpont Morgan Library, 18

Pinckney, Charles Cotesworth, 6

Pine, Robert Edge: portrait of JM attributed to, 151

Placide, A., 103

Pleasants, J. Hall: on Wattles's portrait of JM, 85

Pleasants, Gov. James, 55

Port Folio: Edwin's engraving of JM in, 28

Portraits lost or unlocated: originals by or copies after Paul, 28; Wood, 36–37; Harding, 67–68; Martin, 85, 90; Wattles, 85–86; Hughes, 96; Sully, 108; Thompson, 108; Inman, 154; Thayer, 155; Hubard, 168–169, 170; Ford, 179; Greenough, 179; Value, 180

Powers, Hiram: bust of JM by, in U.S. Capitol, 181, illustrated, 182

Prescott, William Hickling: bust of, by Frazee, 172

Price, Mrs. J. Addison, 62

Princeton University Library, 18

Quincy, Eliza Susan, 122

Rains Gallery, 90

Randolph, Innes: repairs damaged bust of JM, 10; presents copy to Richmond Historical Society, 13, illustrated, 12; verses of, on Rogers's statue of JM, 183, 185

Randolph, Dr. Jacob: and his account of JM's operation for the stone, 136–137

Randolph, John, of Roanoke: portrait of, by Harding, 66; at Virginia Constitutional Convention, 113

Rawle, Francis, 154–155

Rawle, William H., 132, 134

Redwood Library and Athenaeum, Newport, R.I., 67

Renshaw, Michael (librarian of the Bar Library Company of Baltimore): on Wattles's portrait of JM, 87

Replica: defined, ix

Reyntiens, Patrick (stained-glass artist): and likeness of JM in Washington Cathedral, 82

Ribble, Dean F. D. G., 163

Rice of Washington: and photographs of Saint-Mémin's drawing, 19

Richmond City Council: procures portrait of JM by R. M. Sully, 101, 103, illustrated, 102

Richmond City Hall: R. M. Sully portrait of JM at, 101, 104, 110

Richmond Compiler: on Harding's portrait of JM, 66; notices Catlin's presence in Richmond, 113–114

Richmond Standard: description of Waugh relief of JM in, 93, illustrated, 94

Richmond *Times-Dispatch:* account of R. M. Sully's portraits of JM in, 101

Richmond *Whig:* advertisement of J. W. Ford's portrait of JM in, 179

Ringold, Tench, 149

Roan, William, 55

Roberts, Rev. W. T. (rector of Bruton Parish Church), 79
Robertson, Mrs. Harrison (granddaughter of JM), 169
Robinson, Agnes, 152
Robinson, Conway, 111
Rodman, Thomas H., 31
Roe, Philip L., 151
Rogers, John: engraving of JM after Inman by, 158, illustrated, 159
Rogers, Randolph: statue of JM by, 183, illustrated, 184
Roseberg, Carl A.: designs medal of JM, 191, illustrated, 190
Rosenthal, Albert: engraving of JM after Jarvis by, 62, illustrated, 60; etching of JM after Harding by, 80, illustrated, 81
Rousuck, E. J., 42, 44
Ruckle, Thomas C., 85, 87
Rueff, André, 33
Ruffin, Mrs. Ellen (granddaughter of JM): on Saint-Mémin's JM, 24; on Inman's replica of JM, 139, 141
Rust, Thomas A.: persuades JM to sit to Martin, 83–84

Saint-Mémin, Charles Balthazar Julien Fevret de, 4, 5, 18
    likenesses of JM by: original drawing at Duke University, 19, illustrated, 20; photoengraving by Klackner, 21–22, illustrated, 22; engraved reproductions, 23–24, illustrated, 24; drawing as model for Hall of Fame medal, 26, 34, illustrated, 25
Sartain, John, 144, 146
Savage, Edward, 4, 28
Schachner, Nathan: Jarvis portrait of JM in *Aaron Burr: A Biography* by, 55
Schlecht, Charles, 146
Schley, Buchanan, 90
Schley, M. Sullivan, 58
Seals: likenesses of JM on, 188, 191, illustrated, 190
Selden, Mrs. Lynde, 33

Shades. *See chap. 16 on Brown's silhouettes*
Sharples, James, 4
Silvette, David: portrait of JM after W. D. Washington by, 162, 163, illustrated, 162; portrait of JM as a Mason by, 185, illustrated, 187
Sizer, Theodore, 58
Slavin, John: portrait of JM after Inman by, 146, illustrated, 148
Smibert, John, 1
Smith, Angelice K., 143
Smith, Ellen Harvie, 45
Smith, Mrs. Ellen Page, 10
Smith, Frank Bulkely, 165
Smith, George D., 192
Smith, Thomas Marshall, Jr.: on Saint-Mémin's JM, 19; corresponds with J. B. Thayer, 21; sells Saint-Mémin's JM, 23
Smith, Mrs. Thomas Marshall (Margaret Marshall, granddaughter of JM), 19
Soule, Charles C. (lawbook seller of Boston), 24
Spark, Victor: owner of copy of so-called Houdon bust, 13; owner of R. M. Sully's sketch of JM, 103; owner of Hubard portrait of JM, 165
Spofford, Ainsworth R. (librarian of Congress), 131
Springfield Republican: evaluation of Harding as artist in, 64
Stain, Joseph, 151
Stanford School of Law: and its portrait of JM, 151, illustrated, 150
State Department. *See* United States Department of State
State Historical Society of Wisconsin: R. M. Sully portrait of JM at, 101, 104, 106, 110, 112, illustrated, 107
Staunton, Virginia, Circuit Courthouse: R. M. Sully portrait of JM at, 101, 104, 110, 111
Staunton Spectator: account of Sully's JM at Circuit Court of Staunton in, 104

Stevens, Benjamin F., 120
Stevenson, Mrs. Robert H., Jr., 90
Storm King Art Center, Mountain-ville, N.Y., 42n
Story, Justice Joseph, 129; likeness of, in Morse's *Old House of Representatives,* 41; JM presents Harding portrait to, 65; bequeaths Harding JM to Harvard, 67; writes sketch of JM for *National Portrait Gallery,* 139; bust of, by Frazee, 171; JM presents bust by Frazee to, 175
Story, William Wetmore: statues of JM by, 129, 131–132, illustrated, 131, 132
Stuart, Gilbert, 1, 4, 118, 142, 158
Sully, Robert Matthew, 3, 4, 127; JM's recommendation of, 100–101; at Virginia Constitutional Convention, 113
   portraits of JM by: in Richmond City Hall, 101, 103, illustrated, 102; owned by Victor Spark, 103, 104, illustrated, 105; at State Historical Society of Wisconsin, 104, 106, 108, illustrated, 107; at Corcoran Gallery of Art, 108, illustrated, 109; at Virginia Museum of Fine Arts, 110–111, illustrated, 110
Sully, Thomas, 4, 100, 104
Supreme Court of the United States: portrait of JM by Martin at, 87, 92, illustrated, 88; bust by Hughes at, 97, illustrated, 97
Surget, Mrs. Eustace, 69, 70
Sutherland, Arthur E., 178
Swan, Mabel M.: on Harding's JM at Boston Athenaeum, 74
Swann, Mrs. Mary Marshall, 13
Swift, Gen. Joseph Gardner: portrait of, by Jarvis, 54

Talleyrand-Périgord, Charles M. de, 6
Taney, Chief Justice Roger B., 144
Thayer, Ezra B., 155

Thayer, James B., 19, 21, 59, 64, 158; correspondence of, with Horace Gray, 69; correspondence of, with E. E. Hall, 74; discovers origin of Harvard's replica of Harding's Athenaeum JM, 77–78; correspondence of, on R. M. Sully's JM at Corcoran, 108; on Inman's JM, 134
Thayer, Dr. John Marshall: owner of Jarvis portrait of JM, 57, illustrated, 57
Thayer, Theodora W. (daughter of J. B. Thayer): copy of Inman's JM by, 154–155
Thayer, William B., Jr., 57
Thayer, Mrs. William B., 57
Thayer, Dr. William S., 19
Thomas, Douglas H., 90, 92, 125
Thomas, John Gregg, 167
Thomas Gilcrease Institute of American History and Art: owner of Jarvis's portrait of JM, 58–59, illustrated, 59
Thompson, Cephas, 3, 4, 26, 30, 37; sits on bench with JM, 27
   portraits of JM by or after: at Johns Hopkins University, 28, illustrated, 29; at Association of the Bar of the City of New York, 31, illustrated, 32; at John Marshall House, 31, illustrated, 33; at Bowdoin College Museum of Art, 33, illustrated, 33
Trumbull, John, 1, 4, 40, 113, 115, 139; mistaken attribution of Jarvis portrait of JM to, 58
Tulane University, New Orleans: owner of Harding portrait of JM, 69, 70, illustrated, 70
2300 Club, Richmond, Va.: Jarvis portrait of JM on loan to, 58, illustrated, 34

Union League of Philadelphia: owner of J. R. Lambdin's portrait of JM, 149, illustrated, 150

United States Bureau of Engraving and Printing: R. Peale's porthole portrait of JM reproduced by, 50, illustrated, 50

United States Capitol: W. W. Story's statue of JM at, 129, illustrated, 132; Brooke's portrait of JM at, 161, 163, illustrated, 161; Power's bust of JM at, 181, illustrated, 182

United States Departmest of State: Inman's portrait of JM on loan to, 138; E. F. Andrews's copy of Inman's JM at, 154

United States House of Representatives. See *Old House of Representatives, The*

United States Supreme Court. See Supreme Court of the United States

University Club, New York City: owner of portrait of JM, 58, illustrated, 57

University of Virginia: owner of Martin portrait of JM, 83, 92, illustrated, 84; owner of Hubard portrait of JM, 164, 165, illustrated, 167

Valentine Museum, Richmond: portrait of JM at, 58, illustrated, 59

Value, Jane: lost portrait of JM by, 180

Vanderbilt, William H., 13

Van Schaick, Mrs., 192

Vaughan, John, 100

Vauthier, Moreau: reproduction of so-called Houdon bust of JM by, 14, 15, illustrated, 14

Villard, Mrs. Oswald Garrison: former owner of miniature of "dearest Polly," 8

Virginia Colonization Society: JM chairman of, 143

Virginia Constitutional Convention, 1829–1830, 4, 113; Harding at, 66; R. M. Sully at, 100, 109–110; Catlin at, 113; Harding's description of, 114; J. W. Ford at, 179; Catlin's painting of, illustrated, 116, 117, 119

Virginia General Assembly: declines to purchase Catlin's painting, 118

Virginia Historical Society, 13, 104, 106, 108, 125; Waugh's relief of JM at, 93, illustrated, 94; Catlin's *Virginia Constitutional Convention* at, 120, illustrated, 119; Meyers's JM after Inman at, 147, illustrated, 148; Hubard portrait of JM at, 160, 170, illustrated, 170; portrait of JM by unknown artist at, 180, illustrated, 181

Virginia Law Weekly, 162–163

Virginia Museum of Fine Arts: R. Peale portrait of JM at, 52, illustrated, 51; R. M. Sully portrait of JM at, 110, illustrated, 110

Virginia State Bar Association, 25

Virginia State Capitol Building: bust of JM by Frazee in, 178

Virginia State Library, 48; owner of Inman's replica of JM, 146, 158

Voltaire, François Marie Arouet de: bust of, by Houdon, 16

Wade, Ellen Harvie, 24

Waite, Chief Justice Morrison R., 131, 144

Wallis, Mrs. Miriam E., 97

Walters Art Gallery, Baltimore: and diary of George A. Lucas, 13

Ward, Thomas W. (treasurer of the Boston Athenaeum), 174

Warren, Joseph, 133

Warrenton, Virginia, Courthouse: burning of, 161

Washington, Bushrod: first president of the American Colonization Society, 142

Washington, George, 6, 41, 104, 192; Marshall's *Life* of, 9, 77; statue of, by Houdon, 9; bust of, by Houdon, 15; R. Peale's porthole portrait of, 48; Brown's silhouette of, 125

Washington, William D.: portrait of JM by, 158, 161–162, illustrated, 160

Washington, D.C. *See* Corcoran Gallery of Art; Library of Congress; National Gallery of Art; National Portrait Gallery; Supreme Court of the United States; United States Capitol; United States Department of State; White House, The

Washington and Lee University: portrait of JM by Harding at, 31, 67, illustrated, 69

Washington Cathedral: and its Christian Statement window, 82

Washington University: Cranch portrait of JM at, 71, illustrated, 71; portrait of JM by or after Martin at, 88, 92, illustrated, 90

Wattles, James L.: portrait of JM attributed to, 87, 89, 92, illustrated, 86

Waugh, Beverley, 3, 127; wax bas-relief of JM by, 93, 96, 98–99, illustrated, 94, 95

Webb, John Sidney, 108

Webster, Daniel, 66, 67, 76; Martineau's comment on, 52; portrait of, by Hubard, 164; bust of, by Frazee, 171–172

Weddell, Alexander W., 12, 120

Welch, Thomas B., engraving of JM after Inman by, 156, illustrated, 157

Weldon, Felix G. W. de: bust of JM by, 191

Wellington, Arthur Wellesley, 1st duke of, 2

West, Benjamin, 40

Westmoreland County, Virginia, Courthouse: Frazee bust of JM at, 178

White, Margaret E. (daughter of Harding), 76

White, William A., 163

White Cloud (Indian chief): portrait of, by R. M. Sully, 104

White House, The: Jarvis portrait of JM at, 59, 61, illustrated, 60

Whitney, J. H. E. (engraver), 21

Wickham, John, 55

Wiggin, Albert H., 33

Wilbank, William T.: as treasurer of Marshall Memorial Fund, 129

Wildenstein Gallery, 42

Willard, Joseph: librarian of the Massachusetts Historical Society, 77

William and Mary, College of: and bust of JM by F. de Weldon at, 191. *See also* Marshall-Wythe School of Law

Williams, Alfred Brockenbrough, 10

Williams, John Langborne: presents Martin portrait of JM to University of Virginia, 83

Willing, Edward S., 152

Willing, J. Barton, 154

Wiltshire, William E.: owner of pastel of "dearest Polly," 7–8, illustrated, 8

Winston, Thomas W., 120

Winthrop, Robert C., 114

Wirt, William, 37; portrait of, by Harding, 66; on JM's appearance, 134

Wisconsin Magazine of History, 108

Wood, Joseph: portrait of JM by, 35–37; engraved by Kearny, 35; other likenesses by, 37n

Woodruff, Mrs. Benjamin T.: owner of miniature of JM, 6–7, illustrated, 7

Wythe, George: bust of, by F. de Weldon, 191

XYZ mission, 6

Yale University Art Gallery: owner of portrait of JM, 33, illustrated, 33

Ziegler, Susie L. (granddaughter of Jacob Eichholtz), 143